PRACTICE BOOK 5A

Consultant and author
Dr Fong Ho Kheong

Authors
Gan Kee Soon and Chelvi Ramakrishnan

UK consultants
Carole Skinner, Simon d'Angelo and Elizabeth Gibbs

Published by Marshall Cavendish Education
Times Centre, 1 New Industrial Road, Singapore 536196
Customer Service Hotline: (65) 6213 9688
Email: cs@mceducation.com
Website: www.mceducation.com

Distributed by
Oxford University Press
Great Clarendon Street, Oxford,
OX2 6DP, United Kingdom
www.oxfordprimary.co.uk
www.oxfordowl.co.uk

First published 2015
Reprinted 2015, 2017 (twice), 2018 (twice), 2019 (twice)

ISBN 978-981-01-8896-2

Printed in China

Acknowledgements
Written by Dr Fong Ho Kheong, Chelvi Ramakrishnan and Gan Kee Soon

UK consultants: Carole Skinner, Simon d'Angelo and Elizabeth Gibbs

Cover artwork by Daron Parton

The authors and publisher would like to thank all schools and individuals who helped to trial and review Inspire Maths resources.

Introduction

Inspire Maths is a comprehensive, activity-based programme designed to provide pupils with a firm foundation in maths and to develop the creative and critical thinking skills to become fluent problem solvers.

For the teacher:

Use **Practice** with well-structured questions to check and reinforce concepts learnt in the Pupil Textbook.

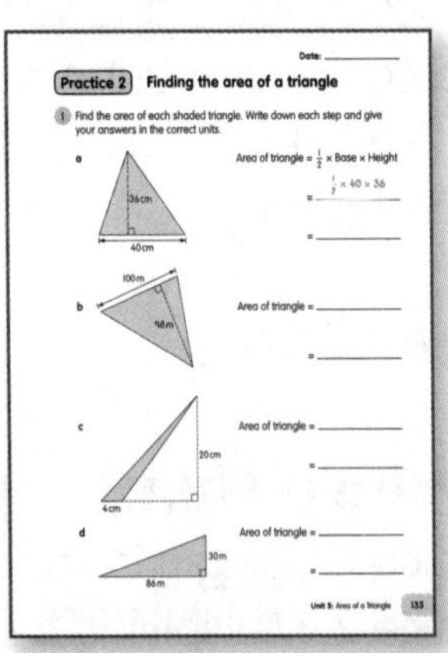

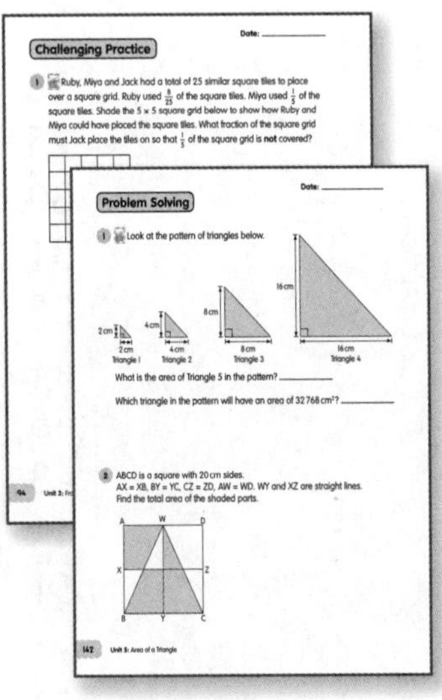

Develop pupils' creativity and critical thinking skills with **Challenging Practice** and **Problem Solving**.

Reviews after every two or three units consolidate the concepts learnt.

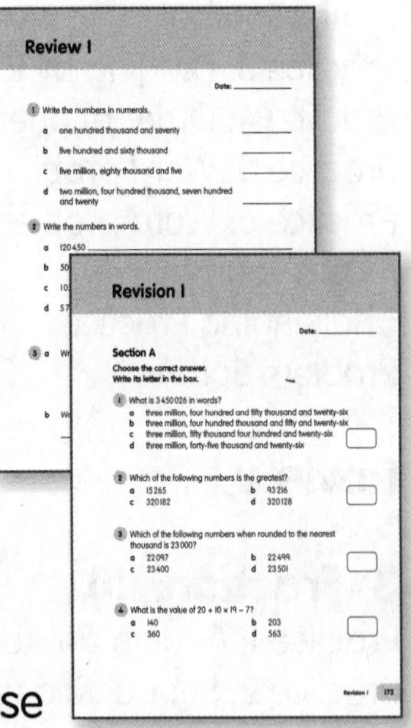

Revisions integrate topics, concepts and strands for complete consolidation.

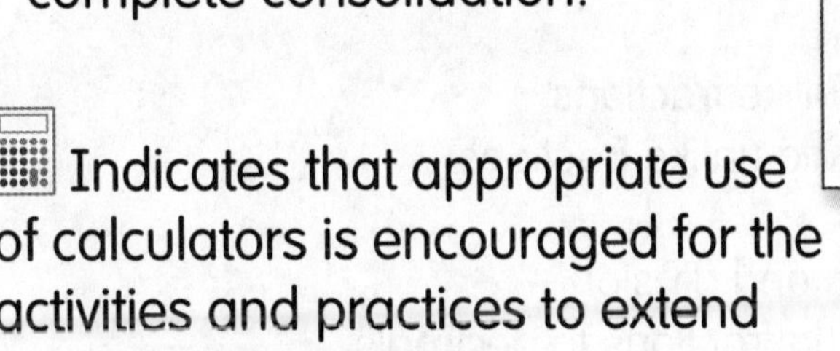 Indicates that appropriate use of calculators is encouraged for the activities and practices to extend problem-solving skills.

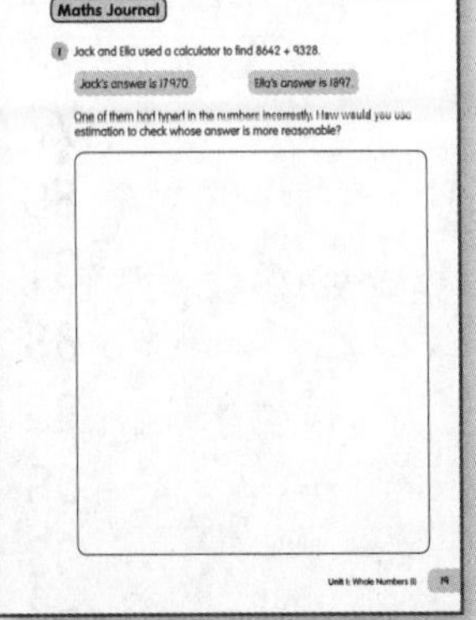

For the pupil:

Share what you have learnt, create your own questions and become aware of your own mathematical thinking in your **Maths Journal**.

Contents

Whole Numbers (I)

Date: ___________________

Practice 1 **Numbers to 10 million**

1 Count in ten thousands or hundred thousands. Then fill in the spaces.

a   80 000, 70 000, 60 000, ________________, ________________

b   100 000, 200 000, 300 000, ________________, ________________

c   900 000, 800 000, 700 000, ________________, ________________

2 Complete the table. Then write the number in numerals and in words.

Hundred Thousands	Ten Thousands	Thousands	Hundreds	Tens	Ones

	In Numerals	In Words
________ hundred thousands	700 000	seven hundred thousand
________ ten thousands		
________ thousands		
________ hundreds		
________ ten		
________ ones		

In numerals, the number is ________________.

In words, the number is ____

____.

3 Write the numbers in numerals.

a

Hundred Thousands	Ten Thousands	Thousands	Hundreds	Tens	Ones

The number is ____________ .

b

Hundred Thousands	Ten Thousands	Thousands	Hundreds	Tens	Ones

The number is ____________ .

c Eight hundred and sixteen thousand, nine hundred and forty-three

____________ .

d Six hundred and five thousand and five hundred ____________ .

e One hundred and three thousand and thirty-one ____________ .

f Eight hundred and seventy thousand and three ____________ .

g Three hundred thousand and twelve ____________ .

h Twenty-two thousand, six hundred and ninety-seven ____________ .

Unit 1: Whole Numbers (I)

4 Fill in the table headings with 'Tens', 'Hundreds', 'Ten Thousands' or 'Hundred Thousands'. Then write the numbers in words.

a

		Thousands			Ones

The number is _______________________________

_______________________________ .

b

		Thousands			Ones

The number is _______________________________

_______________________________ .

5 Write the numbers in words.

65 000: sixty-five thousand
142: one hundred and forty-two

a 65 142 _______________________________

____

b 368 400 _______________________________

____

c 700 070 _______________________________

6 Fill in the spaces with the missing words.

a	Eight hundred and two thousand, one hundred and _______________.	802 101
b	Three hundred and twenty-four _______________, three hundred and six.	324 306
c	One hundred and fifty thousand, _______________ hundred and sixty.	150 260
d	Nine hundred and _______________ thousand, one hundred and _______________.	999 198

7 The populations of some countries are shown below.

Country	Population
Bahamas	46 000
Mauritius	2030
Greenland	56 361
Iceland	299 388
Luxembourg	502 207
Pitcairn Islands	45

a Write the population of Iceland in words.

____

____

b Which country has the smallest population? What is its population?

____

c Which country has a population of about 500 000?

____

Unit 1: Whole Numbers (I)

Practice 2   Numbers to 10 million

1   Write the number in numerals and in words.

Millions	Hundred Thousands	Ten Thousands	Thousands	Hundreds	Tens	Ones

	In Numerals	In Words
_______ millions		
_______ hundred thousands		
_______ ten thousands		
_______ thousands		
_______ hundreds		
_______ tens		
_______ ones		

In numerals, the number is _______________ .

In words, the number is ____

____ .

2 Write the numbers in numerals.

    a   Nine million _______________

    b   Two million, one hundred and fifty-six thousand and four _______________

    c   Five million, two hundred and thirty-eight thousand _______________

    d   Seven million, one hundred and fifty thousand _______________

    e   Six million, sixty thousand and fifty _______________

    f   Three million and three _______________

3 Write the numbers in words.

    a   2 543 000 _______________

    b   5 050 000 _______________

    c   8 147 600 _______________

    d   2 150 000 _______________

    e   7 230 014 _______________

    f   5 192 622 _______________

    g   9 009 009 _______________

Practice 3 — Place and value

1 Fill in the spaces.

Hundred Thousands	Ten Thousands	Thousands	Hundreds	Tens	Ones
●● ●	●● ●●	●●● ●●	●●		●
3	4	5	2	0	1

In 345 201:

a **i** the digit 3 stands for _______________

  ii the value of the digit 3 is _______________

b **i** the digit 4 stands for _______________

  ii the value of the digit 4 is _______________

c **i** the digit 5 stands for _______________

  ii the value of the digit 5 is _______________ .

2 Fill in the boxes with the values of the digits.

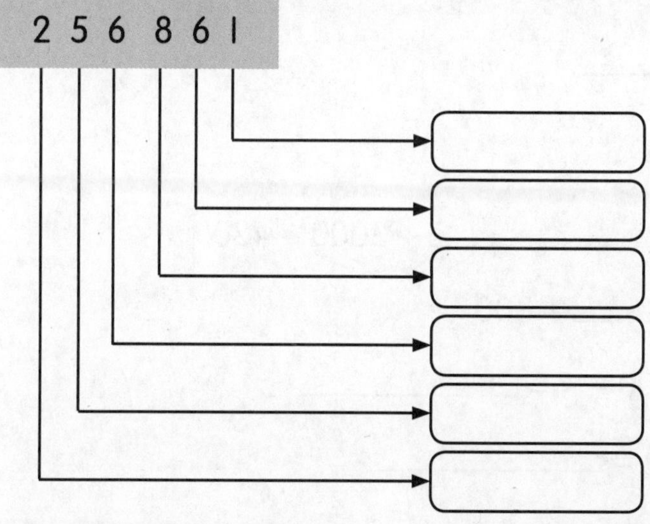

3 In the number 346 812:

    a the digit 3 stands for _______   **b** the digit 6 stands for _______ .

4 What is the value of the digit **2** in each of the numbers below?

    a 329 051 _____________   **b** 903 521 _____________

    c 712 635 _____________   **d** 258 169 _____________

5 Fill in the spaces.

    a In 320 187, the digit _____________ is in the thousands place.

    b In 835 129, the digit 8 is in the _____________________________ place.

    c In 348 792, the digit 4 is in the _____________________________ place.

6 Read the clues to find the number.

> It is a 6-digit number.
> The digit 1 is in the ones place.
> The greatest digit is in the hundred thousands place.
> The value of the digit 5 is 500.
> The digit in the ten thousands place is 3 less than the digit in the hundred thousands place.
> The digit in the thousands place stands for 4000.
> The digit in the tens place is more than 7 but less than 9.

The number is _____________ .

7 Fill in the spaces.

    a 153 420 = 100 000 + _____________ + 3000 + 420

    b 760 300 = _____________ + 300

    c 700 000 + 8000 + 500 + 4 = _____________

    d 200 000 + 2000 + 10 = _____________

8 Fill in the spaces.

Millions	Hundred Thousands	Ten Thousands	Thousands	Hundreds	Tens	Ones
1	5	0	8	3	6	9

In 1 508 369:

a **i** the digit 1 stands for _____________

    ii the value of the digit 1 is _____________

b **i** the digit 8 stands for _____________

    ii the value of the digit 8 is _____________

c the digit 0 is in the _____________________________ place.

9 Fill in the boxes with the values of the digits.

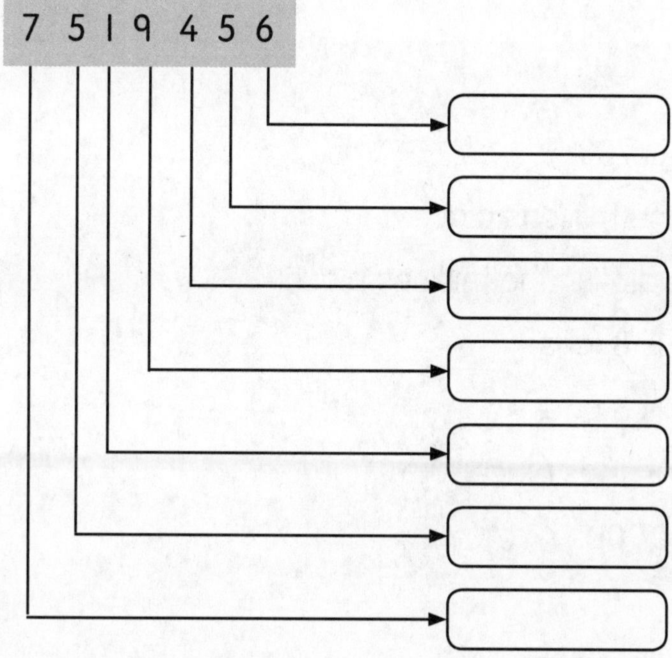

10 Fill in the spaces.

  a   In 5 420 000, the digit 5 is in the _________________________ place.

  b   In 1 077 215, the digit in the hundred thousands place is

  ___________ .

  c   In 9 400 210, the digit 9 stands for ___________ .

  d   4 130 000 = ___________ + 100 000 + 30 000

  e   6 123 750 = 6 000 000 + 123 000 + ___________

  f   7 550 100 = 7 000 000 + ___________ + 100

  g   5 000 000 + 200 000 + 7000 + 70 = ___________

11 Read the clues to find the number.

> It is a 7-digit number.
>
> The value of the digit 7 is 700.
>
> The greatest digit is in the millions place.
>
> The digit 1 is next to the digit in the millions place.
>
> The value of the digit 8 is 8 tens.
>
> The value of the digit 3 is 3 ones.
>
> The digit 5 is in the thousands place.
>
> The digit 6 stands for 60 000.

The number is ___________ .

   Unit 1: Whole Numbers (1)

Practice 4   **Comparing numbers within 10 million**

1 Which is greater, 97 210 or 125 302? Write the values in the place value chart to compare.

Hundred Thousands	Ten Thousands	Thousands	Hundreds	Tens	Ones

__________ hundred thousand is greater than __________ ten thousands.

So __________ is greater than __________ .

2 Circle the smaller number.

   a   128 758 or 74 906   **b**   523 719 or 523 689

3 Circle the greater number.

   a   712 400 or 89 000   **b**   635 002 or 635 100

4 Circle the smallest number and cross (✗) out the greatest number.

375 061   172 503   127 503   157 203   371 560   371 605

5 Arrange the numbers in order, beginning with the smallest.

   a   739 615, 795 316, 315 679, 615 379

____

   b   245 385, 805 342, 97 632, 300 596

____

6 Look at the two numbers in the place value charts and fill in the spaces.

a

Millions	Hundred Thousands	Ten Thousands	Thousands	Hundreds	Tens	Ones
1	0	7	9	7	2	0
	9	9	0	3	9	5

____________ hundred thousands is smaller than ________ million.

So ______________ is smaller than ______________.

b

Millions	Hundred Thousands	Ten Thousands	Thousands	Hundreds	Tens	Ones
1	0	8	3	9	5	2
5	0	9	6	3	5	7

______________ is greater than ______________.

c

Millions	Hundred Thousands	Ten Thousands	Thousands	Hundreds	Tens	Ones
6	4	1	2	5	8	6
6	4	3	8	6	7	1

______________ is greater than ______________.

Unit 1: Whole Numbers (I)

7 Circle the greater number.

    a   4 015 280 or 2 845 000   **b**   999 098 or 1 000 000

8 Circle the smaller number.

    a   2 007 625 or 2 107 625   **b**   7 405 319 or 905 407

9 Arrange the numbers in order, beginning with the greatest.

    a   2 432 000, 480 000, 2 720 000, 3 190 000

    ____

    b   513 900, 3 150 000, 913 000, 2 020 000

    ____

10 What is the next number in each pattern? Fill in the spaces.

    a   738 561, 938 561, 1 138 561, …

        i   938 561 is _____________ more than 738 561.

        ii   1 138 561 is _____________ more than 938 561.

        iii _____________ more than 1 138 561 is _____________.

        The next number in the pattern is _____________.

    b   4 655 230, 4 555 230, 4 455 230, …

        i   4 555 230 is _____________ less than 4 655 230.

        ii   4 455 230 is _____________ less than 4 555 230.

        iii _____________ less than 4 455 230 is _____________.

        The next number in the pattern is _____________.

11 Complete the number patterns. Give the rule for each pattern.

a 230 180, 231 180, 232 180, ______________, ______________

    i 231 180 is ______________ more than 230 180.

    ii 232 180 is ______________ more than 231 180.

    Rule: ____

b 850 400, 845 400, 840 400, ______________, ______________

    Rule: ____

c 2 650 719, 3 650 719, 4 650 719, ______________, ______________

    Rule: ____

d 6 298 436, 5 198 436, 4 098 436, ______________, ______________

    Rule: ____

12 Fill in the spaces. Then solve the riddle below.

a 5 083 000 = 5 000 000 + ______________   **M**

b 5 000 000 + 600 000 + 2000 = ______________   **T**

c Which is greater, 509 900 or 562 000? ______________   **S**

d Which is smaller, 1 020 000 or 1 002 000? ______________   **A**

e The value of the digit 1 in 7 120 000 is ______________.   **P**

f Complete the number pattern. 508 900, 509 000, 509 100, …

    The next number is ______________.   **K**

What goes around the world but remains in the corner?

______	______	______	______	______
562 000	5 602 000	1 002 000	83 000	100 000

Practice 5   Rounding to the nearest thousand and estimating

1 Look at the number lines. Fill in the numbers in the boxes.

a

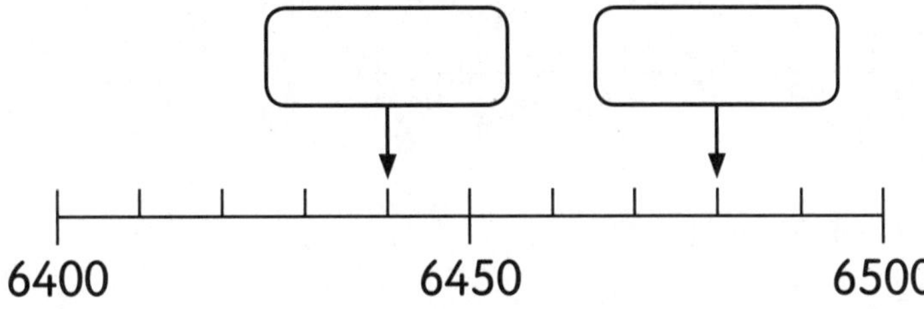

b

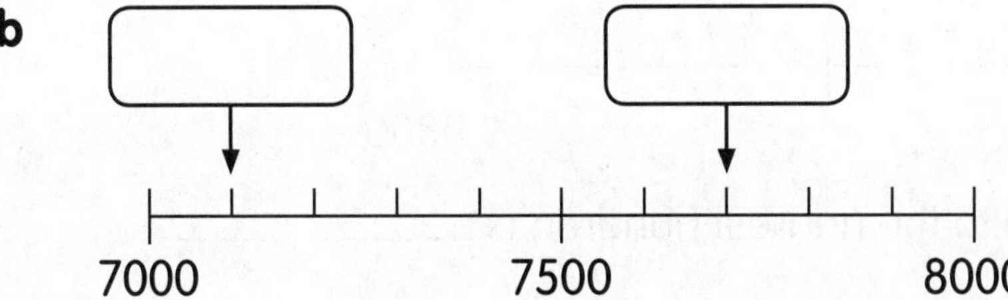

c

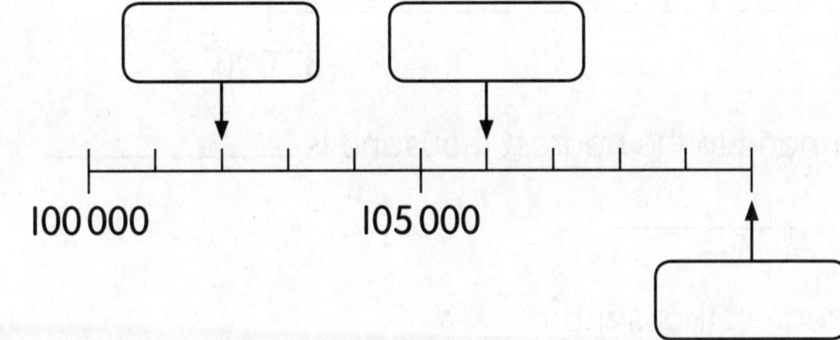

2 Mark the given number with a cross (X) on the number line. Then round the number as specified.

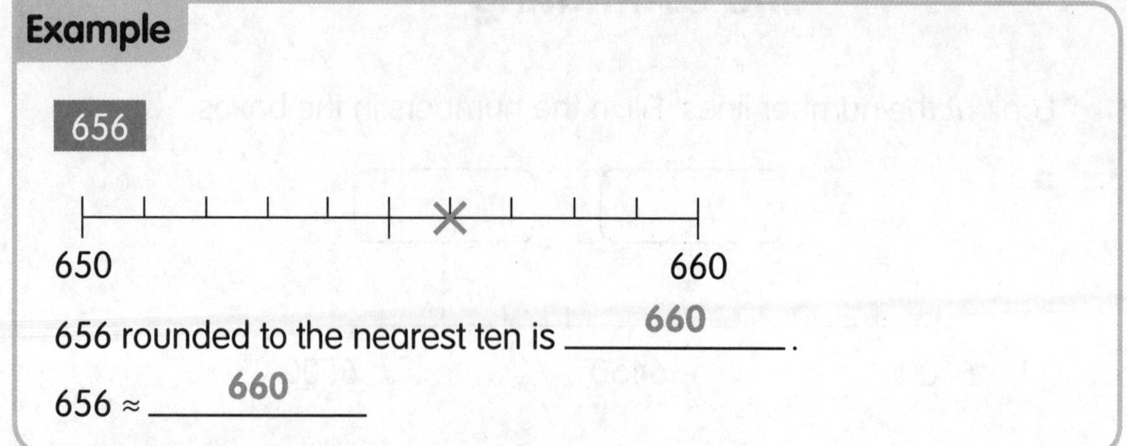

Example

656

650   660

656 rounded to the nearest ten is **660**.

656 ≈ **660**

a 9709

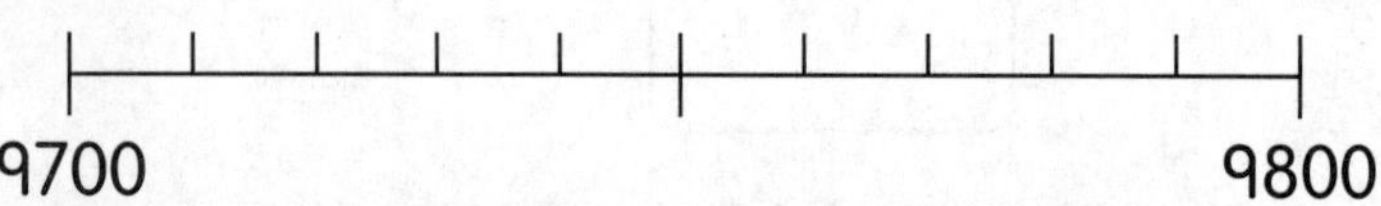

9700   9800

9709 rounded to the nearest hundred is __________.

9709 ≈ __________

b 31 600

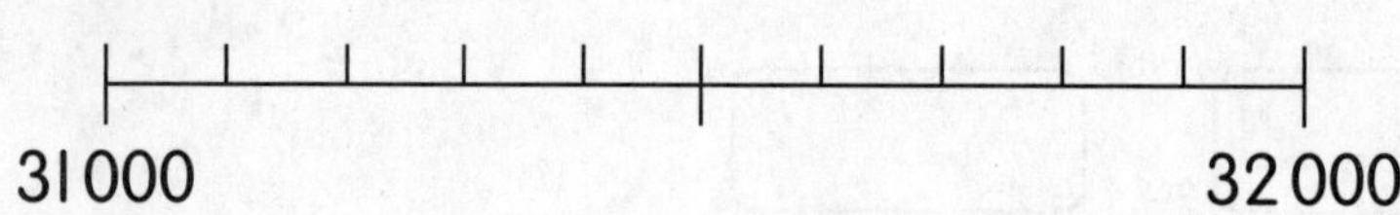

31 000   32 000

31 600 rounded to the nearest thousand is __________.

31 600 ≈ __________

3 Round to the nearest thousand.

a 5637 ≈ __________   **b** 9541 ≈ __________

c 1399 ≈ __________   **d** 72 245 ≈ __________

e 473 075 ≈ __________   **f** 69 547 ≈ __________

g 20 100 ≈ __________   **h** 756 715 ≈ __________

4 Estimate the sum by first rounding each number to the nearest thousand.

a 9286 + 5703 ≈ =	**b** 6789 + 4200 ≈ =
c 7264 + 7153 ≈ =	**d** 4885 + 6075 ≈ =
e 3105 + 9940 ≈ =	**f** 7083 + 2607 ≈ =

5 Estimate the difference by first rounding each number to the nearest thousand.

a 8156 − 6109 ≈ =	**b** 4924 − 4127 ≈ =
c 7105 − 3940 ≈ =	**d** 4885 − 1075 ≈ =

6 Estimate the product by first rounding the 4-digit number to the nearest thousand.

a $\quad 4512 \times 2 \approx$ $\quad\quad\quad = $	**b** $\quad 3765 \times 7 \approx$ $\quad\quad\quad = $
c $\quad 2521 \times 5 \approx$ $\quad\quad\quad = $	**d** $\quad 5108 \times 6 \approx$ $\quad\quad\quad = $
e $\quad 8497 \times 9 \approx$ $\quad\quad\quad = $	**f** $\quad 6060 \times 3 \approx$ $\quad\quad\quad = $

7 Estimate the quotient.

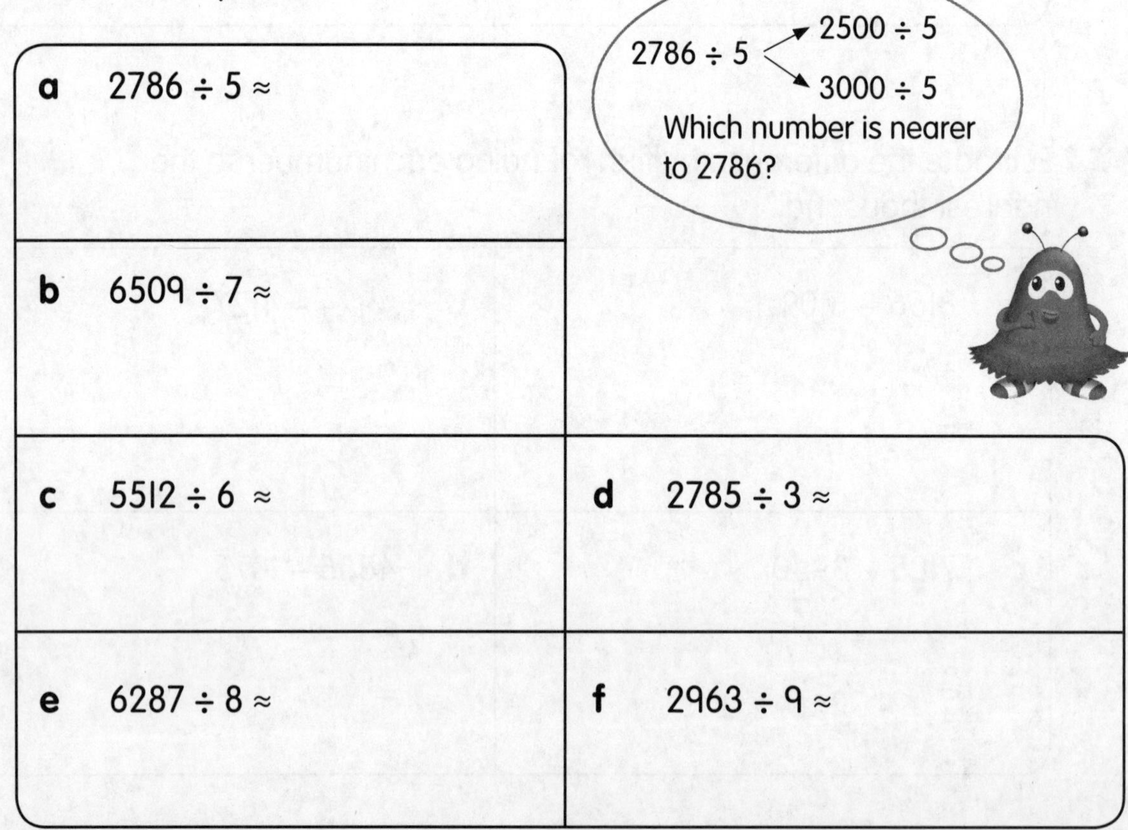

a $\quad 2786 \div 5 \approx$	
b $\quad 6509 \div 7 \approx$	
c $\quad 5512 \div 6 \approx$	**d** $\quad 2785 \div 3 \approx$
e $\quad 6287 \div 8 \approx$	**f** $\quad 2963 \div 9 \approx$

Maths Journal

1. Jack and Ella used a calculator to find $8642 + 9328$.

Jack's answer is 17 970.

Ella's answer is 1897.

One of them had typed in the numbers incorrectly. How would you use estimation to check whose answer is more reasonable?

2 Millie did the following for her homework.

   a $7986 \div 8 = 998 \text{ r } 2$ **b** $2659 \div 3 = 264 \text{ r } 3$

She was asked to check her answers. Show what she would do to check how reasonable her answers are in **a** and **b**.

a

b

Unit I: Whole Numbers (I)

Challenging Practice

1 Arrange the digits below to make three possible 6-digit numbers which are 756 000 when rounded to the nearest thousand.

| 2 | 5 | 5 | 6 | 7 | 8 |

Problem Solving

1 The number 3200 has the digit 3 in the thousands place and the digit 2 in the hundreds place. What number must you subtract from 3200 so that the answer is a 4-digit number with the digit 2 in the thousands place, the digit 3 in the hundreds place and zeros in the tens and ones places?

2 A 3-digit number when divided by 5 gives an even number. When it is divided by 3, it also gives an even number.

    a   What is the digit in the ones place?

    b   What can the number be?

Whole Numbers (2)

Date: _______________

Practice 1 **Using a calculator**

1 Add.

   a $215 + 9843 =$ _______

   b $6789 + 18 =$ _______

   c $97 + 8154 =$ _______

   d $1693 + 8157 =$ _______

2 Subtract.

   a $8215 - 79 =$ _______

   b $6286 - 129 =$ _______

   c $2159 - 1998 =$ _______

   d $26\,145 - 9354 =$ _______

3 Multiply.

   a $359 \times 12 =$ _______

   b $217 \times 58 =$ _______

   c $1975 \times 5 =$ _______

   d $7050 \times 8 =$ _______

4 Divide.

   a $504 \div 9 =$ _______

   b $4104 \div 6 =$ _______

   c $8160 \div 85 =$ _______

   d $17\,604 \div 18 =$ _______

5 Trace Peter's path by finding the values of the following:

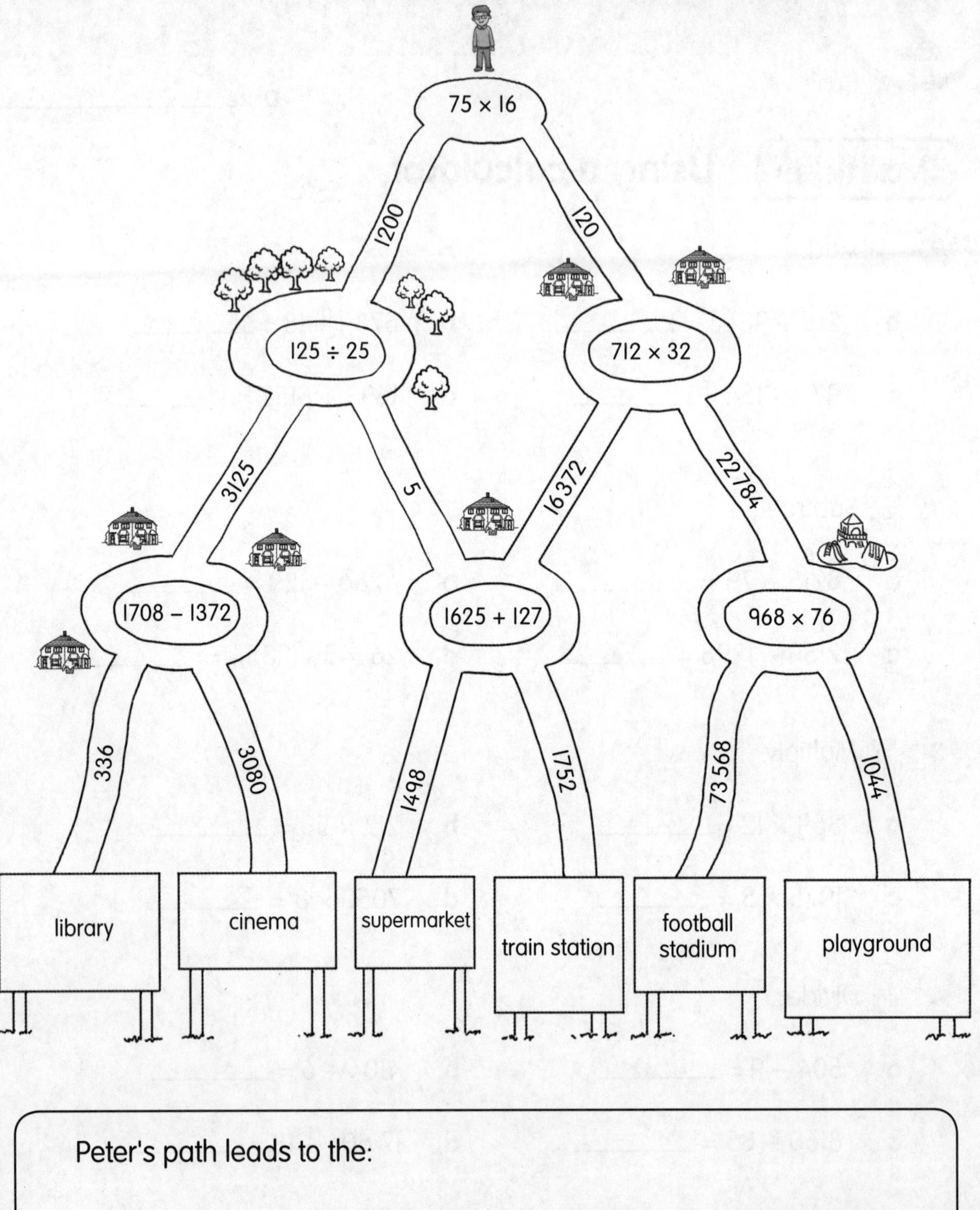

Peter's path leads to the:

____ .

Practice 2 — Multiplying by tens, hundreds or thousands

1 Find the values of the following:

a $47 \times 10 =$ _______________

b $109 \times 10 =$ _______________

c $7140 \times 10 =$ _______________

d $1503 \times 10 =$ _______________

e $3702 \times 10 =$ _______________

f $9342 \times 10 =$ _______________

2 Fill in the spaces.

a $96 \times$ _______________ $= 960$

b _______________ $\times 10 = 700$

c $514 \times$ _______________ $= 5140$

d _______________ $\times 10 = 91\ 760$

e $308 \times$ _______________ $= 3080$

f _______________ $\times 10 = 5000$

3 Fill in the spaces.

a
$$65 \times 40 = 65 \times \underline{\quad} \times 10$$
$$= \underline{\quad} \times 10$$
$$= \underline{\quad}$$

b
$$39 \times 30 = 39 \times \underline{\quad} \times 10$$
$$= \underline{\quad} \times 10$$
$$= \underline{\quad}$$

c
$$120 \times 50 = 120 \times \underline{\quad} \times \underline{\quad}$$
$$= \underline{\quad} \times \underline{\quad}$$
$$= \underline{\quad}$$

d
$$143 \times 90 = 143 \times \underline{\quad} \times \underline{\quad}$$
$$= \underline{\quad} \times \underline{\quad}$$
$$= \underline{\quad}$$

e
$$360 \times 30 = 360 \times \underline{\quad} \times \underline{\quad}$$
$$= \underline{\quad} \times \underline{\quad}$$
$$= \underline{\quad}$$

f
$$285 \times 80 = 285 \times \underline{\quad} \times \underline{\quad}$$
$$= \underline{\quad} \times \underline{\quad}$$
$$= \underline{\quad}$$

4 Multiply.

25 × 100 =	**M**	7 × 1000 =	**T**
86 × 100 =	**P**	70 × 1000 =	**E**
95 × 100 =	**A**	400 × 1000 =	**L**
217 × 100 =	**P**	726 × 1000 =	**H**
803 × 100 =	**C**	8032 × 1000 =	**O**
3810 × 100 =	**B**	3936 × 1000 =	**S**

What is this cat's name? Match the letters above to the answers below to find out.

P						
21 700	9500	7000	80 300	726 000	70 000	3 936 000

5 Fill in the spaces.

a 17 × _________ = 1700

b _________ × 1000 = 25 000

c _________ × 1000 = 478 000

d 320 × _________ = 320 000

e 1315 × _________ = 131 500

f _________ × 1000 = 2 662 000

6 Fill in the spaces.

a 4×300

$= 4 \times \underline{\hspace{1.5cm}} \times 100$

$= \underline{\hspace{1.5cm}} \times 100$

$= \underline{\hspace{2.5cm}}$

b 12×500

$= 12 \times \underline{\hspace{1.5cm}} \times 100$

$= \underline{\hspace{1.5cm}} \times 100$

$= \underline{\hspace{2.5cm}}$

c 35×600

$= 35 \times \underline{\hspace{1.5cm}} \times 100$

$= \underline{\hspace{1.5cm}} \times 100$

$= \underline{\hspace{2.5cm}}$

d 814×700

$= 814 \times \underline{\hspace{1.5cm}} \times 100$

$= \underline{\hspace{1.5cm}} \times 100$

$= \underline{\hspace{2.5cm}}$

e 5400×800

$= 5400 \times \underline{\hspace{1.5cm}} \times 100$

$= \underline{\hspace{1.5cm}} \times 100$

$= \underline{\hspace{2.5cm}}$

f 8×5000

$= 8 \times \underline{\hspace{1.5cm}} \times 1000$

$= \underline{\hspace{1.5cm}} \times 1000$

$= \underline{\hspace{2.5cm}}$

g 12×3000

$= 12 \times \underline{\hspace{1.5cm}} \times 1000$

$= \underline{\hspace{1.5cm}} \times 1000$

$= \underline{\hspace{2.5cm}}$

h 15×2000

$= 15 \times \underline{\hspace{1.5cm}} \times 1000$

$= \underline{\hspace{1.5cm}} \times 1000$

$= \underline{\hspace{2.5cm}}$

i 300×4000

$= 300 \times \underline{\hspace{1.5cm}} \times 1000$

$= \underline{\hspace{1.5cm}} \times 1000$

$= \underline{\hspace{2.5cm}}$

j 663×6000

$= 663 \times \underline{\hspace{1.5cm}} \times 1000$

$= \underline{\hspace{1.5cm}} \times 1000$

$= \underline{\hspace{2.5cm}}$

7 Answer these questions.

	Multiplying by Tens	Multiplying by Hundreds	Multiplying by Thousands
a	$17 \times 70 =$	$17 \times 700 =$	$17 \times 7000 =$
b	$65 \times 30 =$	$65 \times 300 =$	$65 \times 3000 =$
c	$90 \times 40 =$	$90 \times 400 =$	$90 \times 4000 =$
d	$812 \times 10 =$	$812 \times 100 =$	$812 \times 1000 =$
e	$634 \times 20 =$	$634 \times 200 =$	$634 \times 2000 =$

8 Fill in the spaces.

    a $31 \times \underline{\hspace{2cm}} = 3100$ **b** $30 \times \underline{\hspace{2cm}} = 90\,000$

    c $103 \times \underline{\hspace{2cm}} = 3090$ **d** $25 \times \underline{\hspace{2cm}} = 5000$

 Unit 2: Whole Numbers (2)

9 Imagine you are the owner of an electronics shop. Estimate the amount of earnings you will get from the sales of each group of items below.

> 58 all-in-one printers at £219 each.
> 652 digital radios at £73 each.
> 99 games consoles at £217 each.
> 39 plasma television sets at £4156 each.
> 13 computers at £2415 each.
> 37 home entertainment systems at £6814 each.

Round the 2-digit numbers to the nearest ten, the 3-digit numbers to the nearest hundred and the 4-digit numbers to the nearest thousand. Then estimate the product.

a $58 \times 219 \approx$ ________ $\times$ ________

$=$ ________

b $652 \times 73 \approx$ ________ $\times$ ________

$=$ ________

c $99 \times 217 \approx$ ________ $\times$ ________

$=$ ________

d $39 \times 4156 \approx$ ________ $\times$ ________

$=$ ________

e $13 \times 2415 \approx$ ________ $\times$ ________

$=$ ________

f $37 \times 6814 \approx$ ________ $\times$ ________

$=$ ________

Maths Journal

1. Use your calculator to work out:

$$1164 \times 97$$

Explain how you can check if your answer is reasonable.

Practice 3 — Dividing by tens, hundreds or thousands

1 Find the values of the following:

a 100 ÷ 10 = __________

b 670 ÷ 10 = __________

c 1050 ÷ __________ = 105

d __________ ÷ 10 = 1974

e 52 260 ÷ 10 = __________

f 30 500 ÷ __________ = 3050

2 Fill in the spaces.

a 5610 ÷ 30 = 5610 ÷ __________ ÷ 3

= __________ ÷ 3

= __________ (J)

b 3000 ÷ 60 = 3000 ÷ 10 ÷ __________

= __________ ÷ 6

= __________ (M)

c 1040 ÷ 40 = 1040 ÷ __________ ÷ __________

= __________ ÷ __________

= __________ (A)

d 8700 ÷ 60 = 8700 ÷ __________ ÷ __________

= __________ ÷ __________

= __________ (T)

e 3450 ÷ 50 = 3450 ÷ __________ ÷ __________

= __________ ÷ __________

= __________ (R)

f 34 230 ÷ 70 = 34 230 ÷ __________ ÷ __________

= __________ ÷ __________

= __________ (N)

What is Ruby's favourite treat? Write the letters which match the answers to find out.

____ ____ ____   ____ ____ ____ ____
187   26   50   145   26   69   145

3 Divide.

3400 ÷ 100 =	**P**	560 000 ÷ 1000 =	**H**
5000 ÷ 100 =	**S**	38 000 ÷ 1000 =	**I**
7700 ÷ 100 =	**N**	360 000 ÷ 1000 =	**M**
2000 ÷ 100 =	**B**	415 000 ÷ 1000 =	**A**

Which group of animals does the frog belong to? Write the letters which match the answers to find out.

$\overline{}\ \overline{}\ \overline{}\ \overline{}\ \overline{}\ \overline{}\ \overline{}\ \overline{}\ \overline{}\ \overline{}$
415   360   34   560   38   20   38   415   77   50

4 Divide.

a 300 ÷ 300 = 300 ÷ ___ ÷ ___ = ___ ÷ ___ = ___	**b** 1600 ÷ 400 = 1600 ÷ ___ ÷ ___ = ___ ÷ ___ = ___
c 81 000 ÷ 900 =	**d** 45 000 ÷ 500 =
e 9000 ÷ 3000 =	**f** 56 000 ÷ 7000 =

g 60 000 ÷ 400 =	**h** 31 500 ÷ 500 =
i 36 000 ÷ 4000 =	**j** 150 000 ÷ 2000 =
k 133 000 ÷ 7000 =	**l** 120 000 ÷ 8000 =

5 Answer these questions.

	Dividing by Tens	Dividing by Hundreds	Dividing by Thousands
a	1190 ÷ 70 =	11 900 ÷ 700 =	119 000 ÷ 7000 =
b	1950 ÷ 30 =	19 500 ÷ 300 =	195 000 ÷ 3000 =
c	3600 ÷ 40 =	36 000 ÷ 400 =	360 000 ÷ 4000 =
d	12 680 ÷ 20 =	126 800 ÷ 200 =	1 268 000 ÷ 2000 =

6 Fill in the spaces.

a 430 ÷ _______ = 43   **b** 9000 ÷ _______ = 30

c 49 000 ÷ _______ = 7   **d** 2400 ÷ _______ = 120

e 64 000 ÷ _______ = 160   **f** 85 000 ÷ _______ = 17

A national cycle route runs from the Trent and Mersey Canal to Wisbech.
Colour the numbers below that match the answers above to find out the
cycle route number.

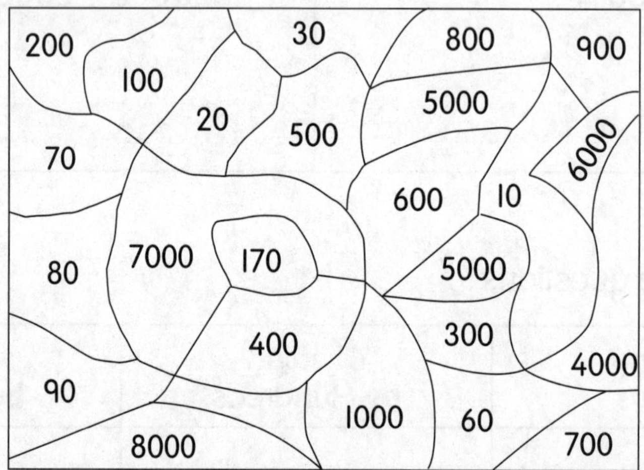

7 Estimate the quotient.

a 6452 ÷ 27 ≈ _______ ÷ _______   **b** 7865 ÷ 41 ≈ _______ ÷ _______

= _______   = _______

c 9125 ÷ 345 ≈ _______ ÷ _______   **d** 9825 ÷ 206 ≈ _______ ÷ _______

= _______   = _______

e 7226 ÷ 871 ≈ _______ ÷ _______   **f** 5299 ÷ 49 ≈ _______ ÷ _______

= _______   = _______

   Unit 2: Whole Numbers (2)

Practice 4 — Order of operations

1 Find the value of each of the following. Write down each step. Then use your calculator to check your answers.

a 18 − 11 − 4 = _______

Step 1: ___ 18 − 11 = 7 ___

Step 2: _______________

b 26 + 8 − 19 = _______

Step 1: _______________

Step 2: _______________

c 12 + 16 − 9 + 3 = _______

Step 1: _______________

Step 2: _______________

Step 3: _______________

d 58 − 23 + 11 − 6 = _______

Step 1: _______________

Step 2: _______________

Step 3: _______________

2 Find the value of each of the following. State the order of operations.

		Order
a	12 + 14 + 9 =	+ +
b	60 + 18 − 7 =	
c	26 − 12 + 7 =	
d	70 − 15 − 49 =	
e	23 + 16 − 7 + 12 =	
f	15 − 12 + 17 − 6 =	

3 Find the value of each of the following. Write down each step. Then use your calculator to check your answers.

a $9 \times 6 \div 2 =$ ______

Step 1: _______________

Step 2: _______________

b $25 \times 3 \div 5 =$ ______

Step 1: _______________

Step 2: _______________

c $200 \div 10 \times 3 \div 5 =$ ______

Step 1: _______________

Step 2: _______________

Step 3: _______________

d $250 \div 5 \div 10 \times 2 =$ ______

Step 1: _______________

Step 2: _______________

Step 3: _______________

4 Find the value of each of the following. State the order of operations.

		Order
a	$30 \times 2 \times 5 =$	✕ ✕
b	$6 \times 10 \div 5 =$	
c	$28 \div 7 \times 4 =$	
d	$40 \div 8 \div 5 =$	
e	$20 \div 10 \times 8 \div 2 =$	
f	$120 \div 12 \div 2 \times 16 =$	

5 Find the value of each of the following. Write down each step. Then use your calculator to check your answers.

a $7 \times 8 - 6 =$ _______

Step 1: _______________

Step 2: _______________

b $14 + 9 \times 7 =$ _______

Step 1: _______________

Step 2: _______________

c $200 \div 20 + 5 =$ _______

Step 1: _______________

Step 2: _______________

d $80 - 16 \div 4 =$ _______

Step 1: _______________

Step 2: _______________

6 Find the value of each of the following. State the order of operations.

		Order
a	$25 - 5 \times 3 =$	$\times$ $-$
b	$90 + 16 \div 8 =$	
c	$83 - 72 \div 6 =$	
d	$5 + 90 \times 7 =$	
e	$240 \div 20 + 15 =$	
f	$7 \times 80 - 160 =$	

7 Find the value of each of the following. Write down each step. Then use your calculator to check your answers.

a $54 \div 6 + 20 \times 4 =$ _______

Step 1: _______________

Step 2: _______________

Step 3: _______________

b $40 - 6 + 10 \times 3 =$ _______

Step 1: _______________

Step 2: _______________

Step 3: _______________

c $36 \div 6 - 25 \div 5 =$ _______

Step 1: _______________

Step 2: _______________

Step 3: _______________

d $25 \times 4 - 36 \div 9 =$ _______

Step 1: _______________

Step 2: _______________

Step 3: _______________

8 Find the value of each of the following. State the order of operations.

		Order
a	$60 \div 3 + 14 \times 2 =$	$\div \; \times \; +$
b	$20 - 5 \times 2 + 6 =$	
c	$13 - 6 \times 2 + 12 \div 4 =$	
d	$27 \div 3 + 40 \times 6 =$	
e	$64 - 60 + 12 \times 3 =$	
f	$42 \div 7 - 2 + 7 =$	

9 Find the value of each of the following. Write down each step. Then use your calculator to check your answers.

a $(15 - 11) \times 9 =$ _______

Step 1: _______________

Step 2: _______________

b $(11 + 5) \div 16 =$ _______

Step 1: _______________

Step 2: _______________

c $63 - (9 \times 7) =$ _______

Step 1: _______________

Step 2: _______________

d $32 \div (14 + 2) =$ _______

Step 1: _______________

Step 2: _______________

10 Find the value of each of the following. State the order of operations.

			Order
a	$3 \times 72 \div 8 =$		$\div$ $\times$
b	$40 \div 5 \times 11 =$		
c	$(36 - 15) \times 2 =$		
d	$36 - 15 \times 2 =$		
e	$(62 + 10) \div 6 =$		
f	$70 \div (16 - 9) =$		

11 Find the value of each of the following. Write down each step. Then use your calculator to check your answers.

a $21 + (12 + 6) \div 3 =$ ______

Step 1: _____________

Step 2: _____________

Step 3: _____________

b $7 + (8 - 4) \times 10 =$ ______

Step 1: _____________

Step 2: _____________

Step 3: _____________

c $32 \div (7 + 1) \times 9 - 5 =$ ______

Step 1: _____________

Step 2: _____________

Step 3: _____________

Step 4: _____________

d $(47 + 12) - 10 \div 5 \times 3 =$ ______

Step 1: _____________

Step 2: _____________

Step 3: _____________

Step 4: _____________

12 Find the value of each of the following. State the order of operations.

		Order
a	$100 + (720 + 200) \div 2 =$	$(+) \div +$
b	$24 \times 5 - (125 - 80) =$	
c	$60 \div (5 + 7) \times 20 - 30 =$	
d	$11 + (34 + 16) \div 5 =$	
e	$7 \times 6 - (18 - 6) =$	
f	$21 \div (2 + 5) \times 12 - 8 =$	

   Unit 2: Whole Numbers (2)

Practice 5   **Word problems (I)**

Solve these word problems. Show your workings clearly.

I   A cricket club had 146 members. Each member paid £30 a month for training fees. How much did the club collect in fees in a year?

2   Mrs Lake has £4500 to buy each person in a group a present.

a   If she can spend £25 on each person, how many people are there in the group?

b   If the presents cost £32 each, how much more money does she need?

3 A group of tourists visited Underwater World. The entrance fees were £13 for each adult and £7 for each child. There were 10 adults and 18 children in the group. How much did they pay altogether?

4 The length of a rectangular wooden plank is 10 cm longer than its width. It is 26 cm wide. The wooden plank is cut into 9 identical pieces. What is the area of each piece of wooden plank?

5 There are 918 yellow chairs and blue chairs altogether in the hall.
The blue chairs are arranged in 36 rows with 12 chairs in each row.
The yellow chairs are arranged in rows of 18. How many rows of yellow chairs are there?

6 The table below shows how much it costs to hire a van.
Gemma hires one from Tuesday to Sunday one week. How much does it cost her?

Weekdays	£56 per day
Saturday and Sunday	£78 per day

7 The table shows the charges at a car park.

First hour	£2
Every additional $\frac{1}{2}$ hour	£1

a Ava parked her car at the car park from 9:30 a.m. to 11:00 a.m. on the same day. How much did she have to pay?

b Serge parked his car there from 9:00 a.m. to 12:30 p.m. on the same day. How much did he have to pay?

 Unit 2: Whole Numbers (2)

Practice 6 — Word problems (2)

Solve these word problems. Show your workings clearly.

1. Mr Elm and Mr Castro have £120. Mr Elm and Miss Wilson have £230. Miss Wilson has 6 times as much money as Mr Castro. How much money does Mr Elm have?

2. Lewis is 10 years old and his sister is 7 years old. In how many years' time will their total age be 41 years?

3 A box of envelopes and 2 staplers cost £10.
3 boxes of envelopes and 2 staplers cost £18.
Find the total cost of 1 box of envelopes and 1 stapler.

4 Ella and Hardeep had the same number of cards at first. After Ella gave
18 of her cards away, Hardeep had 4 times as many cards as Ella. How
many cards did each child have at first?

5 A basket with 65 plums has a mass of 3200 g. The same basket with 40 plums has a mass of 2125 g. Each plum has the same mass. What is the mass of the basket?

6 A carton can hold 850 cm^3 of apple juice. Miss Roberts wants to buy 15 cartons of apple juice. Every 250 cm^3 of apple juice costs £1. How much does she have to pay altogether?

Maths Journal

1 Write down how you feel about using a calculator for your maths lessons.

____

____

____

____

2 Omar was asked to work out $6 + 4 \times 2$. He worked out the steps like this:

$$6 + 4 \times 2 = 10 \times 2 = 20$$

Is he correct? Explain why.

Challenging Practice

1 A box of raisins cost 15 pence and a packet of 8 similar boxes of raisins cost £1. Carl bought exactly 37 boxes of raisins. What was the least amount of money that Carl spent on the raisins?

2 40 children made some triangles for bunting. One child became unwell so the rest of the children made 3 more triangles each. How many triangles did they make altogether?

3 ▦ Mr Tate puts up poles from one end of a road to the other at equal distances apart. There are 27 wooden poles. The width of each pole is 10 cm. The distance between 2 poles is 3000 cm. Find the length of the road.

4 Tai has 64 coins in his money box. There are 20 pence coins and 50 pence coins. The total value of all the coins is £18·50. How many 20 pence coins and how many 50 pence coins are there?

Problem Solving

1. Miss Robinson, Mr Brown and Miss Clarke share £268. Mr Brown has £20 more than Miss Robinson and Miss Clarke has twice as much money as Mr Brown. How much money do Miss Robinson and Mr Brown have altogether?

2. Joshua and Rachel had the same number of marbles. After Rachel gave away 10 marbles and Joshua gave away 22 marbles, Rachel had 3 times as many marbles as Joshua. How many marbles did each of them have at first?

 George had a total of 30 pens and pencils at first. He then decided to exchange all his pens for pencils. If he exchanged every pen for 2 pencils, he would have 48 pencils. How many pens and pencils did he have at first?

Review 1

Date: ___________

1. Write the numbers in numerals.

   a   one hundred thousand and seventy   ___________

   b   five hundred and sixty thousand   ___________

   c   five million, eighty thousand and five   ___________

   d   two million, four hundred thousand, seven hundred
        and twenty   ___________

2. Write the numbers in words.

   a   120 450 ____

   b   500 312 ____

   c   1 050 400 _______________________________________

   d   5 732 800 _______________________________________

        ____

3. a   Write a 6-digit number with the digit 1 in the ten thousands place.

   b   Write this number in words.

   ____

4 In 1 238 906:

  a   the digit 8 stands for _______________

  b   the digit 6 stands for _______________

  c   the digit 9 stands for _______________

  d   the digit 1 stands for _______________ .

5 What is the value of the digit 3 in the numbers below?

  a   538 426: _______________   **b**   1 325 407: _______________

6 Fill in the spaces.

  a   In 807 456, the digit _______ is in the thousands place.

  b   In 5 486 302, the digit _______ is in the millions place.

  c   In 305 128, the digit 0 is in the _______________ place.

  d   In 7 614 892, the digit 6 is in the _______________ place.

7 Fill in the spaces.

  a   918 230 = _______________ + 10 000 + 8000 + 200 + 30

  b   538 417 = 500 000 + _______________ + 8000 + 400 + 10 + 7

  c   6 000 000 + 30 000 + 90 = _______________

  d   128 531 = 100 000 + 20 000 + 8000 + 500 + 30 + 1

        = _______________ + 500 + 31

        = 128 000 + _______________

8 Fill in the spaces with **greater than** or **smaller than**.

  a   185 263 is _______________ 183 256.

  b   5 060 345 is _______________ 995 863.

  c   899 506 is _______________ 900 650.

  d   231 623 is _______________ 231 621.

9 Arrange these numbers in order, beginning with the greatest.

528 010   1 280 500   62 815   258 100   528 100

____

10 What is the next number in the pattern? Fill in the spaces.

276 300, 286 300, 296 300, …

286 300 is __________ more than 276 300.

286 300 is __________ less than 296 300.

__________ more than 296 300 is __________ .

The next number is __________ .

11 Estimate the values of the following:

a $7512 + 3281 \approx$ _______________________________

b $6528 - 5938 \approx$ _______________________________

c $1592 \times 5 \approx$ _______________________________

d $2576 \div 3 \approx$ _______________________________

12 A 4-digit number when rounded to the nearest thousand is 5000.

a   What is the smallest possible number? __________________

b   What is the greatest possible number? __________________

13 Make a 6-digit number using all the cards shown for each of the following. Do **not** start with the digit 0.

| 5 | 0 | 1 | 4 | 9 | 6 |

a   An odd number: _________________.

b   An even number: _________________.

c   A number with the digit 0 in the thousands place: _________________.

d   A number beginning with the greatest digit: _________________.

e   A number with the digit 6 in the tens place and the digit 5 in the

ones place: _________________.

f   A number ending with the smallest digit: _________________.

g   A number where the digit 1 stands for 100 000 and the digit 9 is

in the ones place: _________________.

h   A number greater than 496 501: _________________.

i   A number where the digit 4 is in the ten thousands place and the

digit 6 stands for 600 000: _________________.

j   The greatest possible number: _________________.

k   The smallest possible number: _________________.

l   The difference between the greatest possible number and the

smallest possible number: _________________.

14 🖩 Answer these questions. Remember to write the correct units in your answers. You may use your calculator where necessary.

a Find the area of a square of which each side is 96 cm.

____

b Mr Jenkins has £5651. Mrs Kim has £853 more than Mr Jenkins. How much does Mrs Kim have?

____

c There is 176 ℓ of petrol in Container A. There is 19 ℓ less petrol in Container B. How many litres of petrol is there in Container B?

____

d The mass of a cake is 2 kg. It is cut into 25 equal pieces. What is the mass of each piece of cake? Give your answer in grams.

____

e What number can be subtracted from 5400, so that the answer has the digit 2 in the thousands place and the digit 3 in the hundreds place?

____

15 Fill in the spaces.

a 315 × 10 = _________

b _________ × 10 = 10 000

c 147 × 50 = _________

d 3050 × 70 = _________

e 25 × 100 = _________

f 25 × 1000 = _________

g _________ × 100 = 506 200

h 9236 × _________ = 9 236 000

i 63 × 200 = _________

j 63 × 2000 = _________

k 906 × 7000 = _________

l 1145 × 600 = _________

16 Fill in the spaces.

a 3560 ÷ 10 = _________

b 81 000 ÷ 10 = _________

c 9150 ÷ _________ = 915

d _________ ÷ 10 = 2050

e 900 ÷ 60 = _________

f 3150 ÷ 70 = _________

g 1900 ÷ 100 = _________

h 17 000 ÷ 1000 = _________

i 3600 ÷ _________ = 36

j _________ ÷ 1000 = 40

k 96 000 ÷ 400 = _________

l 504 000 ÷ 9000 = _________

17 Estimate the values of the following:

a $4593 \div 53 \approx$

b $6298 \div 164 \approx$

c $7623 \div 4451 \approx$

d $4593 \div 73 \approx$

18 Find the value of each of the following.

a	$15 + 90 + 42 =$
b	$60 + 12 - 36 =$
c	$50 - 30 - 12 =$
d	$3 \times 8 \times 5 =$
e	$10 \times 9 \div 3 =$
f	$29 + 42 \div 6 =$
g	$(23 + 40) \div (34 - 25) =$
h	$(90 - 85) \times 7 =$
i	$50 \times 8 + 12 \div 4 =$
j	$69 \div 3 - 3 + 10 =$

Solve these word problems. Show your workings clearly.

19 Tony had an equal number of cheese sandwiches and tuna sandwiches. He sold 66 cheese sandwiches. He had 4 times as many tuna sandwiches as cheese sandwiches left. How many sandwiches did he have at first?

20 Mr Bell had 20 m of material. He made 5 curtains. He used 3 m of material for making each curtain. Then he used 2 m of material to make a cushion cover. How much material did he have left?

21 At a school fair, Mrs Smith's class sold 25 ℓ of orange juice. The orange juice was sold in cups containing 200 ml and 300 ml. An equal number of cups containing 200 ml and 300 ml were sold. How many cups of orange juice did her class sell?

22 Michael used 220 cm of wire to make the shape below.

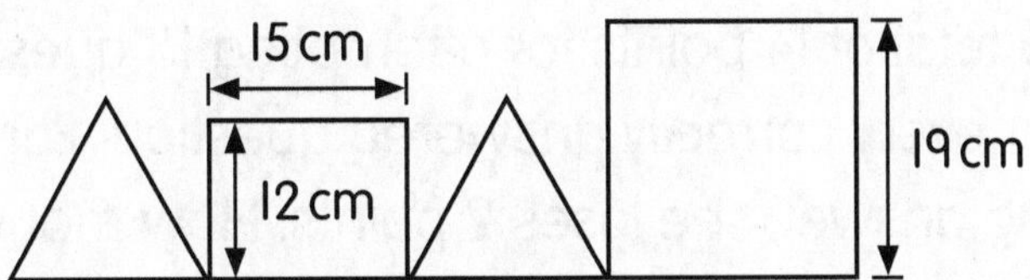

The shape is made up of two identical triangles, a rectangle measuring 15 cm by 12 cm and a square of which each side is 19 cm. What is the length of one side of the triangle if all the sides of the triangle are the same?

23 William bought 260 bags at 5 for £25. He then sold all of them at 2 for £18. How much money did he make?

24 Farha scores a total of 14 points for attempting 15 questions in a maths quiz. For every correctly answered question, Farha gets 2 points. For every wrong answer, she loses 2 points. How many questions has she answered correctly?

25 If Beth feeds her goldfish 14 fish pellets a day, a tin of pellets will last 20 days. If she feeds her goldfish 8 fish pellets a day instead, how many more days will the same tin of pellets last?

26 Miss Barton could pick 8 kg of strawberries per hour at a farm. In the first week, she picked a total of 144 kg of strawberries after some time. Miss Barton was paid £12 per hour for picking strawberries.
  a   How long did she take to pick 144 kg of strawberries?
  b   If she picked the same mass of strawberries in the second week, how much did she earn for both weeks altogether?

27 There are 11 488 residents in the town of Ashton. There are 160 more residents in the town of Greenford. The number of residents in the town of Upside is half the total number of residents in Ashton and Greenford. How many residents are there in Upside?

28 Jasmine mixed 1250 ml of juice with twice as much water to make some lemon squash. She poured the squash equally into 15 glasses. How much lemon squash was there in each glass? Give your answer in millilitres.

Fractions (1)

Date: _______________

Practice 1 **Adding unlike fractions**

1 Find two equivalent fractions for each of the following:

Example

$\dfrac{2}{3} = \dfrac{4}{6} = \dfrac{6}{9}$

a $\dfrac{3}{4} = $ _______ $= $ _______

b $\dfrac{2}{5} = $ _______ $= $ _______

c $\dfrac{5}{6} = $ _______ $= $ _______

2 Express each fraction in its simplest form.

a $\dfrac{6}{8} = $ _______

b $\dfrac{8}{20} = $ _______

c $\dfrac{10}{15} = $ _______

d $\dfrac{9}{21} = $ _______

3 For each pair of fractions, change the denominator of one fraction so that both fractions have the same denominator.

Example

$\dfrac{1}{2}, \dfrac{1}{4}$ $\dfrac{2}{4}, \dfrac{1}{4}$

a $\dfrac{1}{4}, \dfrac{5}{12}$

b $\dfrac{1}{10}, \dfrac{2}{5}$

c $\dfrac{5}{9}, \dfrac{2}{3}$

4 Write equivalent fractions for each fraction below. Then find a common denominator of the fractions.

a $\dfrac{1}{2} = \dfrac{2}{4} =$

    $\dfrac{2}{3} =$

    A common denominator is ______.

b $\dfrac{2}{3} =$

    $\dfrac{3}{4} =$

    A common denominator is ______.

5 a The model has been shaded to show $\dfrac{1}{2}$ and $\dfrac{1}{3}$. Look at the model and complete the addition sentence.

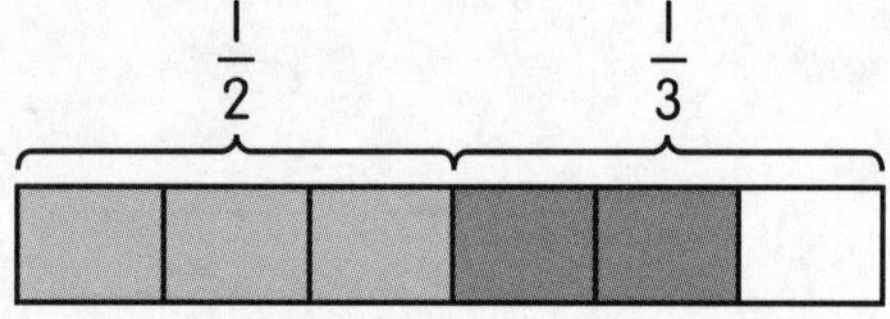

$\dfrac{1}{2} + \underline{\quad\quad} = \dfrac{3}{6} + \underline{\quad\quad}$

$= \underline{\quad\quad}$

b Shade to show $\dfrac{1}{5}$ and $\dfrac{1}{2}$ on the model. Then complete the addition sentence.

$\dfrac{1}{5} + \dfrac{1}{2} = \underline{\quad\quad} + \underline{\quad\quad}$

$= \underline{\quad\quad}$

c Shade to show $\frac{1}{6}$ and $\frac{1}{4}$ on the model. Then complete the addition sentence.

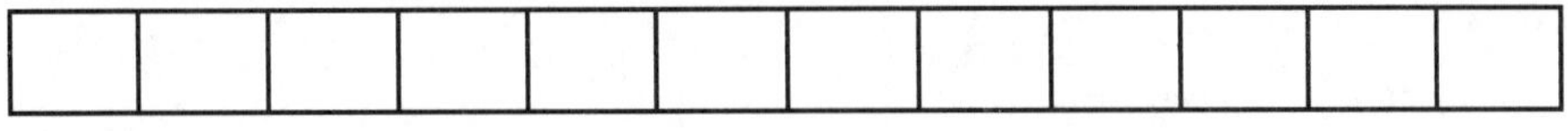

$$\frac{1}{6} + \frac{1}{4} = \underline{\hspace{2cm}} + \underline{\hspace{2cm}}$$

$$= \underline{\hspace{2cm}}$$

d Shade to show $\frac{1}{5}$ and $\frac{2}{3}$ on the model. Then complete the addition sentence.

$$\frac{1}{5} + \frac{2}{3} = \underline{\hspace{2cm}} + \underline{\hspace{2cm}}$$

$$= \underline{\hspace{2cm}}$$

6 Look at the model below. Then write two addition sentences.

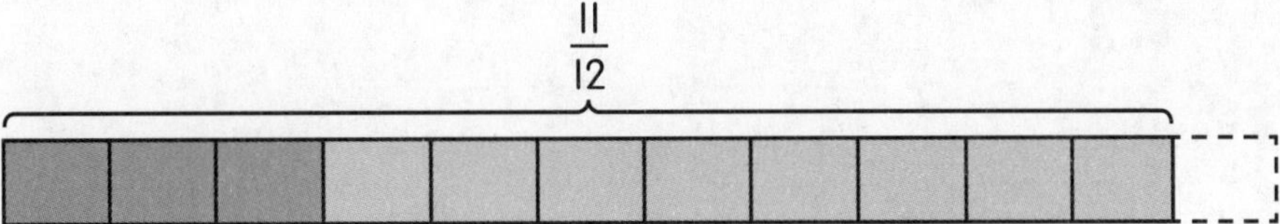

Addition sentence 1:

$$\frac{\boxed{}}{12} + \frac{\boxed{}}{12} = \frac{\boxed{}}{12}$$

Addition sentence 2 (fractions in their simplest form):

$$\underline{\hspace{2cm}} + \underline{\hspace{2cm}} = \underline{\hspace{2cm}}$$

7 Add. Express your answer in its simplest form where necessary.

a $\dfrac{1}{3} + \dfrac{1}{9} =$

b $\dfrac{1}{8} + \dfrac{2}{4} =$

c $\dfrac{1}{3} + \dfrac{3}{8} =$

d $\dfrac{4}{8} + \dfrac{1}{5} =$

e $\dfrac{1}{2} + \dfrac{3}{7} =$

f $\dfrac{1}{6} + \dfrac{3}{10} =$

g $\dfrac{2}{3} + \dfrac{2}{10} =$

h $\dfrac{3}{9} + \dfrac{1}{7} =$

Practice 2 **Subtracting unlike fractions**

1 Here are two fractions: $\frac{1}{2}$ and $\frac{1}{3}$. Convert them to fractions with the same denominator.

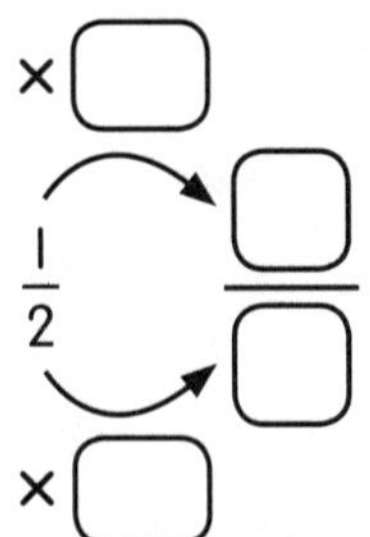

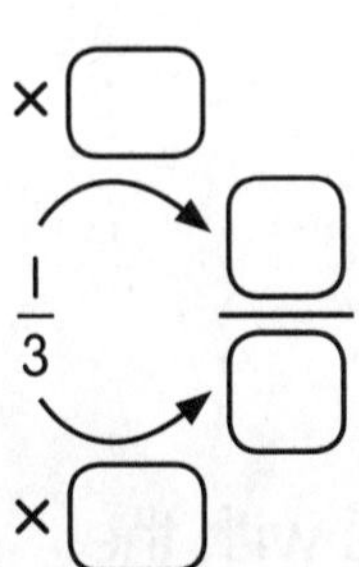

Write the equivalent fractions of $\frac{1}{2}$ and $\frac{1}{3}$ in the boxes.

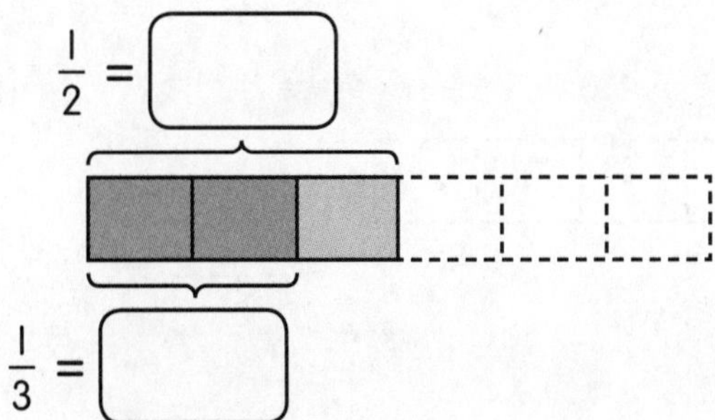

$\frac{1}{2} =$

$\frac{1}{3} =$

Now complete this subtraction sentence.

$$\frac{1}{2} - \frac{1}{3} = \underline{\qquad} - \underline{\qquad}$$

$$= \underline{\qquad}$$

2 Here are two fractions: $\frac{1}{3}$ and $\frac{1}{4}$. Convert them to fractions with the same denominator. Write their equivalent fractions in the boxes.

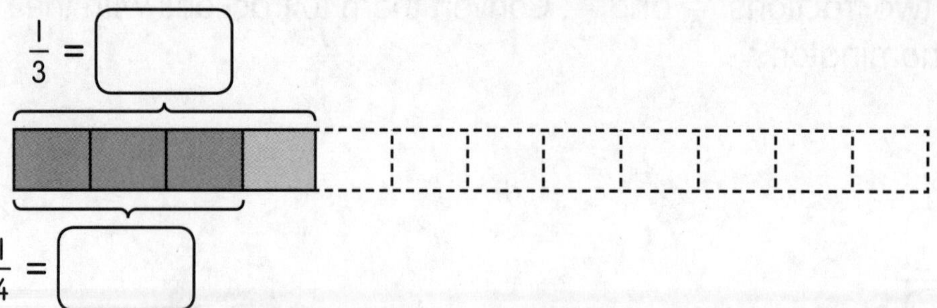

Now complete this subtraction sentence.

$$\frac{1}{3} - \frac{1}{4} = \underline{\hspace{2cm}} - \underline{\hspace{2cm}}$$

$$= \underline{\hspace{2cm}}$$

3 Here are two fractions: $\frac{1}{2}$ and $\frac{1}{5}$. Convert them to fractions with the same denominator. Write their equivalent fractions in the boxes.

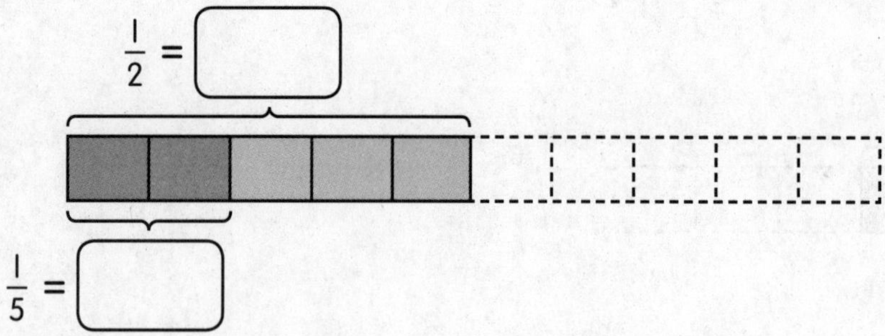

Now complete this subtraction sentence.

$$\frac{1}{2} - \frac{1}{5} = \underline{\hspace{2cm}} - \underline{\hspace{2cm}}$$

$$= \underline{\hspace{2cm}}$$

4 Subtract. Express your answer in its simplest form where necessary.

a $\dfrac{7}{12} - \dfrac{2}{4} =$

b $\dfrac{7}{9} - \dfrac{1}{3} =$

c $\dfrac{5}{6} - \dfrac{1}{12} =$

d $\dfrac{4}{5} - \dfrac{1}{3} =$

e $\dfrac{2}{3} - \dfrac{3}{8} =$

f $\dfrac{7}{9} - \dfrac{1}{4} =$

g $\dfrac{8}{10} - \dfrac{3}{4} =$

h $\dfrac{5}{12} - \dfrac{1}{9} =$

Maths Journal

1 Millie drew a model to find $\frac{4}{5} - \frac{1}{2}$.

She drew the model incorrectly. Explain her mistakes. Then draw the correct model to find the answer.

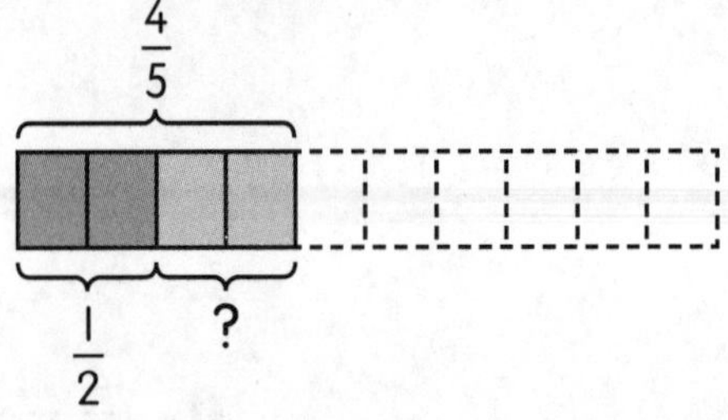

Millie's model is wrong because:

The correct model is:

Practice 3 — Fractions and division

1 Look at the picture. Then write a division sentence and a fraction.

a

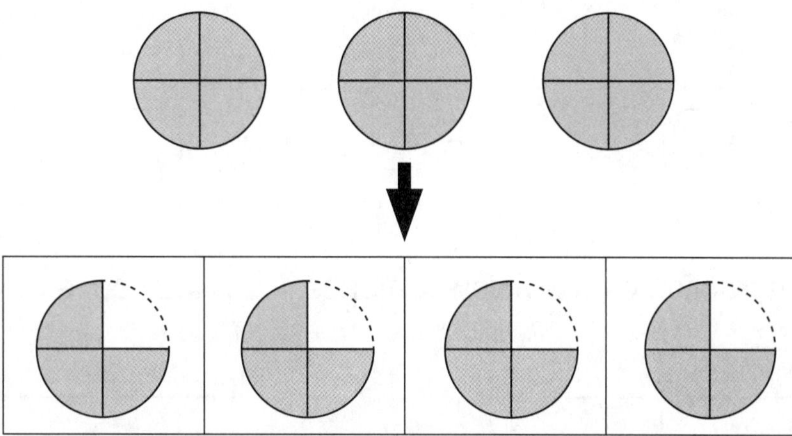

$$3 \div 4 = \frac{\boxed{}}{\boxed{}}$$

b

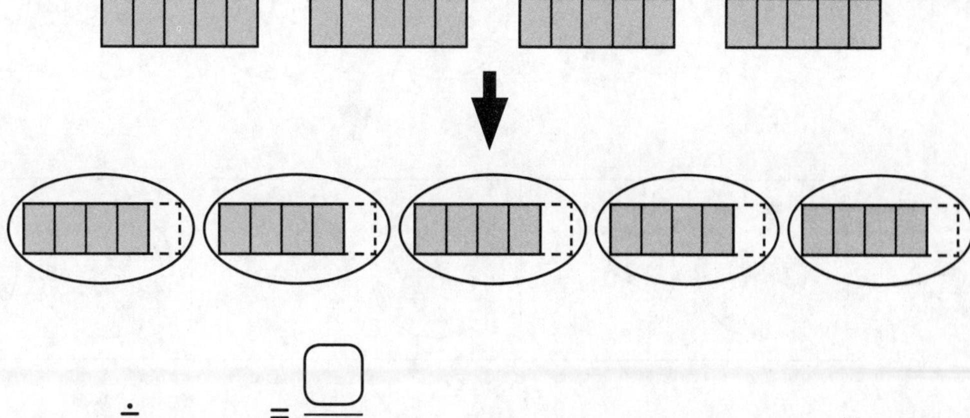

$$\underline{} \div \underline{} = \frac{\boxed{}}{\boxed{}}$$

2 Write each division sentence as a fraction. Fill in the spaces.

a $5 \div 7 = \dfrac{\Box}{\Box}$

b $3 \div 10 = \dfrac{\Box}{\Box}$

c $4 \div 9 = \dfrac{\Box}{\Box}$

d $2 \div 11 = \dfrac{\Box}{\Box}$

3 Write each fraction as a division sentence. Fill in the spaces.

a $\dfrac{7}{8} =$ _______ $\div$ _______

b $\dfrac{5}{12} =$ _______ $\div$ _______

c $\dfrac{1}{10} =$ _______ $\div$ _______

d $\dfrac{6}{7} =$ _______ $\div$ _______

4 Look at the picture. Then write a division sentence, an improper fraction and a mixed number.

a

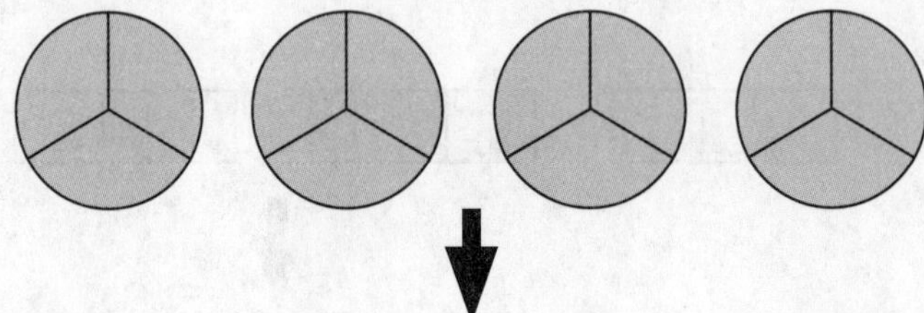

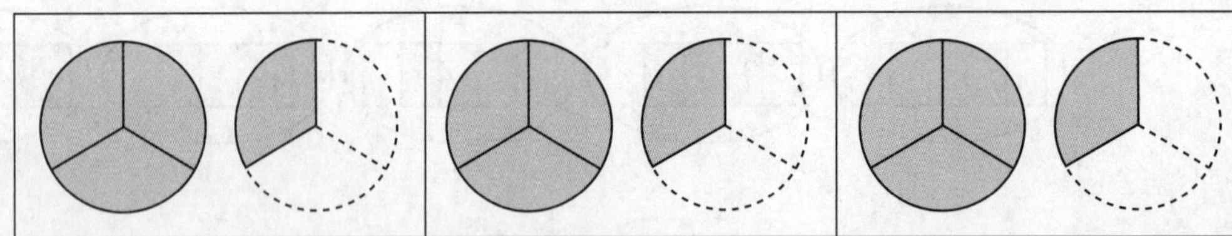

_______ $\div$ _______ $= \dfrac{\Box}{\Box} = \Box\dfrac{\Box}{\Box}$

b

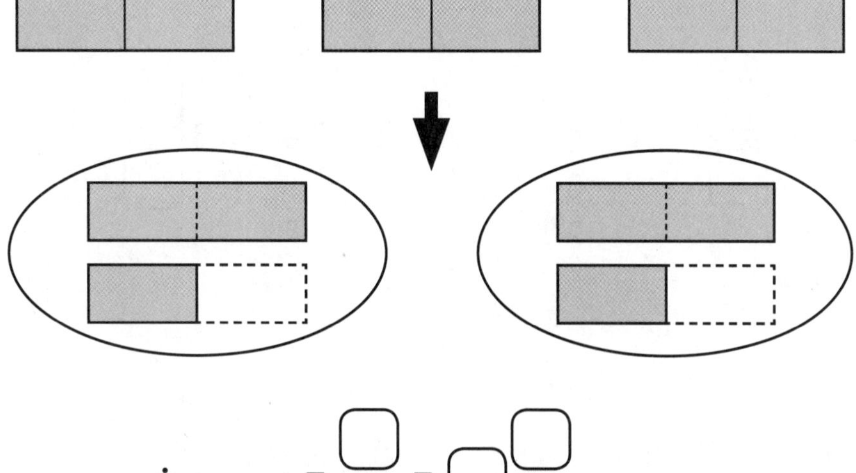

$$\underline{\qquad} \div \underline{\qquad} = \dfrac{\boxed{}}{\boxed{}} = \boxed{}\dfrac{\boxed{}}{\boxed{}}$$

5 Complete the following:

a $\quad 7 \div 4 = \dfrac{\boxed{7}}{\boxed{4}}$

$\qquad = \dfrac{\boxed{4}}{\boxed{4}} + \dfrac{\boxed{}}{\boxed{}}$

$\qquad = 1 + \dfrac{\boxed{}}{\boxed{}}$

$\qquad = \boxed{}\dfrac{\boxed{}}{\boxed{}}$

b $\quad 35 \div 11 = \dfrac{\boxed{}}{\boxed{}}$

$\qquad = \dfrac{\boxed{}}{\boxed{}} + \dfrac{\boxed{}}{\boxed{}}$

$\qquad = 3 + \dfrac{\boxed{}}{\boxed{}}$

$\qquad = \boxed{}\dfrac{\boxed{}}{\boxed{}}$

6 Divide using long division. Express your answer as a mixed number.

a $5 \div 3 = 1\dfrac{\Box}{\Box}$

$$3 \overline{)\ 5}$$
$$\underline{-\ 3}$$
$$2$$

b $7 \div 2 = 3\dfrac{\Box}{\Box}$

c $9 \div 4 =$

d $18 \div 5 =$

7 Write each fraction in its simplest form. Then divide to express your answer as a mixed number.

a $18 \div 4 = \dfrac{\boxed{18}}{\boxed{4}}$

$= \dfrac{\boxed{9}}{\boxed{2}}$

$$2 \overline{)\ 9}$$

$= \Box\dfrac{\Box}{\Box}$

b $22 \div 6 = \dfrac{\Box}{\Box}$

$= \dfrac{\Box}{\Box}$

$= \Box\dfrac{\Box}{\Box}$

 Unit 3: Fractions (I)

Practice 4   Converting fractions to decimals

1 Write each fraction as a decimal.

a $\dfrac{3}{5} = \dfrac{\boxed{}}{\boxed{}}$

= _______

b $\dfrac{13}{20} = \dfrac{\boxed{}}{\boxed{}}$

= _______

c $\dfrac{3}{8} = \dfrac{\boxed{}}{\boxed{}}$

= _______

d $\dfrac{4}{8} = \dfrac{\boxed{}}{\boxed{}}$

= _______

2 Write each fraction as a decimal. Round your answers to 2 decimal places.

a $\dfrac{5}{6} = $ _____ ÷ _____

≈ _______

b $\dfrac{7}{9} = $ _____ ÷ _____

≈ _______

c $\dfrac{4}{7} = $ _____ ÷ _____

≈ _______

d $\dfrac{9}{11} = $ _____ ÷ _____

≈ _______

3 Express each division sentence as an improper fraction and as a decimal correct to 2 decimal places where necessary.

Division Sentence	Express the Division Sentence as:	
	an Improper Fraction	a Decimal
a 8 ÷ 5		
b 7 ÷ 3		
c 12 ÷ 7		

4 Express each division sentence as a mixed number and as a decimal correct to 2 decimal places where necessary.

Division Sentence	Express the Division Sentence as:	
	an Improper Fraction	a Decimal
a $12 \div 5$		
b $7 \div 2$		
c $9 \div 4$		
d $11 \div 6$		

5 Express each improper fraction as a decimal correct to 2 decimal places.

a $\dfrac{40}{15} \approx$ _______

b $\dfrac{53}{13} \approx$ _______

c $\dfrac{43}{21} \approx$ _______

d $\dfrac{65}{17} \approx$ _______

e $\dfrac{65}{14} \approx$ _______

f $\dfrac{35}{13} \approx$ _______

6 Express each mixed number as a decimal correct to 2 decimal places.

a $2\dfrac{3}{21} \approx$ _______

b $5\dfrac{4}{13} \approx$ _______

c $7\dfrac{9}{34} \approx$ _______

d $3\dfrac{5}{17} \approx$ _______

e $4\dfrac{11}{14} \approx$ _______

f $6\dfrac{15}{27} \approx$ _______

7 A coil of rope 217 m long is cut into 9 equal pieces. What is the length of each piece? Express your answer as a mixed number and as a decimal correct to 2 decimal places.

8 A chef bought $8\frac{1}{2}$ kg of apples for £20. Find the cost of 1 kg of apples.

9 Simon bought $47\frac{2}{5}$ kg of meat. He cut the meat into 15 pieces of the same mass. Find the mass of each piece of meat correct to 2 decimal places.

Maths Journal

In a mathematics competition, Daniel and Monica computed the following with their calculators. Circle the incorrect answers. Explain their mistakes.

1

Division	Express the Answer to 2 Decimal Places.	
	Daniel	Monica
$\frac{13}{8}$	1·62	1·63

Reason for the mistake:

2

Division	Express the Answer to 2 Decimal Places.	
	Daniel	Monica
$\frac{14}{9}$	1·56	1·556

Reason for the mistake:

Practice 5 | Adding mixed numbers

1 Add. Express your answer in its simplest form.

a $3\frac{5}{8} + 2\frac{1}{4}$

$$= 3\frac{\boxed{}}{\boxed{}} + 2\frac{\boxed{}}{\boxed{}}$$

$$= 5\frac{\boxed{}}{\boxed{}}$$

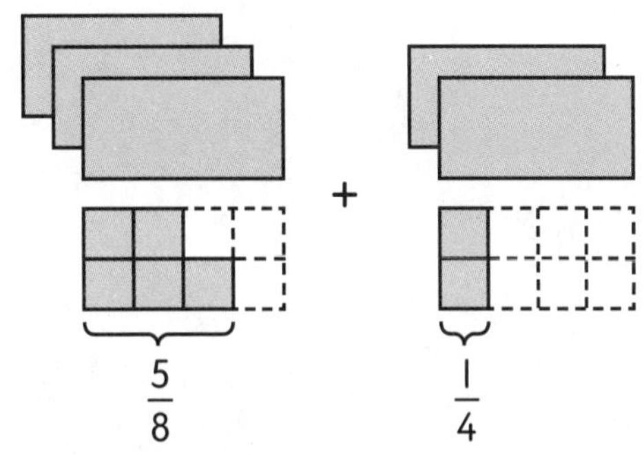

b $1\frac{2}{3} + 2\frac{1}{4}$

$$= 1\frac{\boxed{}}{\boxed{}} + 2\frac{\boxed{}}{\boxed{}}$$

$$= 3\frac{\boxed{}}{\boxed{}}$$

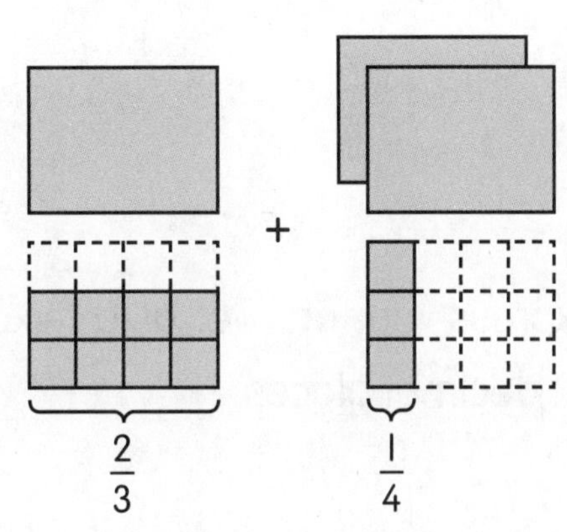

c $2\frac{1}{5} + 3\frac{1}{2}$

$$= 2\frac{\boxed{}}{\boxed{}} + 3\frac{\boxed{}}{\boxed{}}$$

$$= 5\frac{\boxed{}}{\boxed{}}$$

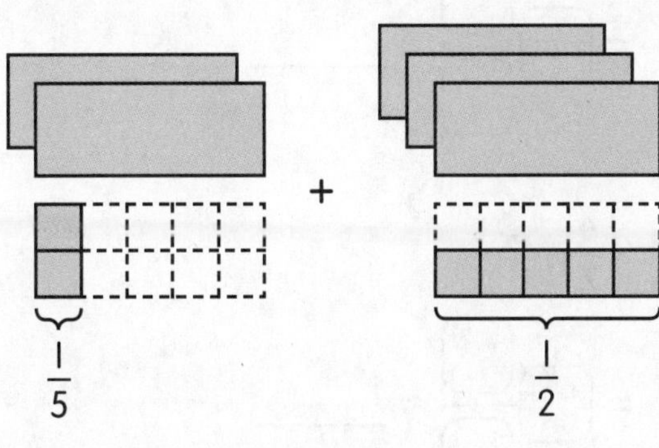

2 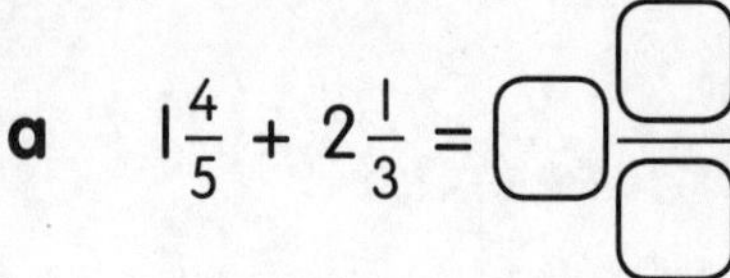 Add. Express your answer in its simplest form.

a $1\frac{4}{5} + 2\frac{1}{3} = \boxed{}\,\dfrac{\boxed{}}{\boxed{}}$

b $3\frac{5}{12} + 1\frac{2}{3}$

c $2\frac{3}{4} + 3\frac{2}{5}$

d $2\frac{5}{9} + 1\frac{5}{6}$

e $4\frac{2}{3} + 2\frac{1}{4}$

f $5\frac{7}{12} + 1\frac{3}{4}$

3 Add. Express your answer as a mixed number and as a decimal correct to 2 decimal places.

a $6\frac{3}{5} + 4\frac{5}{6}$

$= \boxed{}\,\dfrac{\boxed{}}{\boxed{}} \approx \underline{\qquad}$

b $5\frac{7}{8} + 2\frac{2}{7}$

$= \boxed{}\,\dfrac{\boxed{}}{\boxed{}} \approx \underline{\qquad}$

c $9\frac{6}{7} + 7\frac{5}{12}$

$= \boxed{}\,\dfrac{\boxed{}}{\boxed{}} \approx \underline{\qquad}$

d $4\frac{7}{12} + 10\frac{5}{9}$

$= \boxed{}\,\dfrac{\boxed{}}{\boxed{}} \approx \underline{\qquad}$

Practice 6   Subtracting mixed numbers

1 Subtract. Express your answer in its simplest form where necessary.

a $3\frac{2}{3} - \frac{5}{12}$

$$= 3\frac{\boxed{}}{\boxed{}} - \frac{5}{12}$$

$$= 3\frac{\boxed{}}{\boxed{}}$$

$$= 3\frac{\boxed{}}{\boxed{}}$$

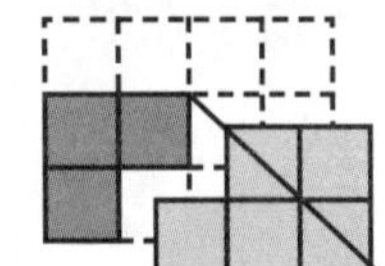

b $4\frac{8}{9} - 3\frac{1}{3}$

$$= 4\frac{8}{9} - 3\frac{\boxed{}}{\boxed{}}$$

$$= 1\frac{\boxed{}}{\boxed{}}$$

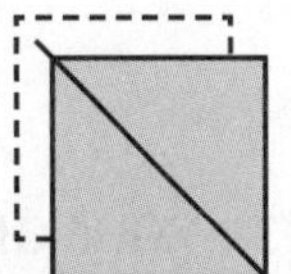
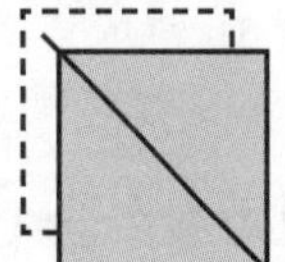
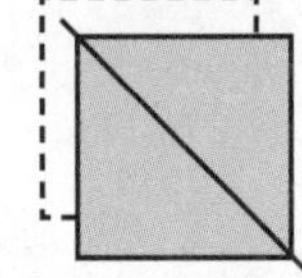
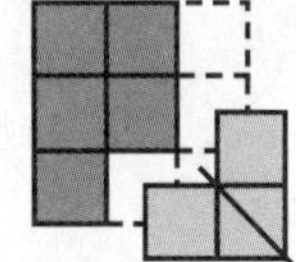

c $3\frac{7}{12} - 2\frac{3}{8}$

$$= 3\frac{\boxed{}}{\boxed{}} - 2\frac{\boxed{}}{\boxed{}}$$

$$= 1\frac{\boxed{}}{\boxed{}}$$

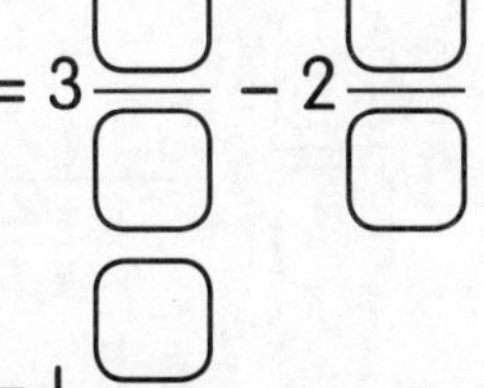

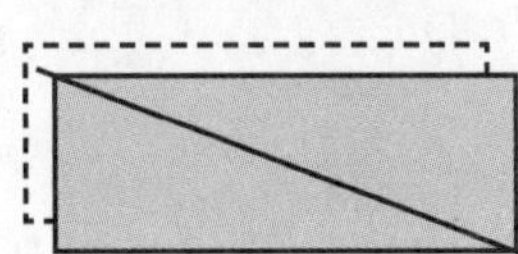
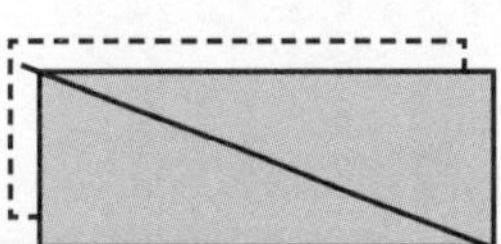
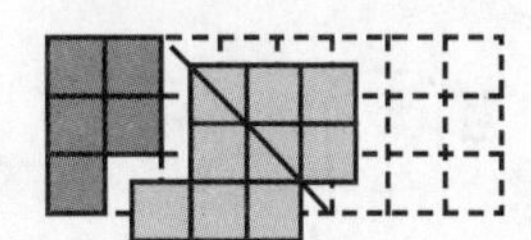

2 Subtract. Express your answer as a mixed number.

a $3\frac{1}{4} - 1\frac{7}{8} =$

b $5\frac{1}{3} - 3\frac{5}{12} =$

c $4\frac{1}{5} - 1\frac{1}{3} =$

d $6\frac{3}{8} - 3\frac{5}{6} =$

e $7\frac{1}{4} - 5\frac{1}{12} =$

f $8\frac{1}{3} - 4\frac{3}{4} =$

3 Subtract. Express your answer as a mixed number and as a decimal correct to 2 decimal places.

a $7\frac{2}{9} - 2\frac{5}{12}$

$= \approx \underline{}$

b $5\frac{2}{7} - 2\frac{7}{8}$

$= \approx \underline{}$

c $12\frac{2}{5} - 8\frac{7}{12}$

$= \approx \underline{}$

d $20\frac{4}{11} - 5\frac{7}{9}$

$= \approx \underline{}$

Practice 7   **Word problems (I)**

Solve these word problems. Show your workings clearly.

1. Rajesh baked 12 flapjacks of the same size. He gave an equal amount of the flapjacks to 5 friends. How many flapjacks did he give each friend?

2. Mrs Little had a ball of string 26 m long. She cut 5 m of string to tie up some parcels. The remaining string was then cut into 4 equal pieces. What is the length of each piece of string?

3 Mr Dee bought 57 kg of sugar. He packed an equal amount of sugar into 6 bags and had 4 kg of sugar left. What is the mass of sugar in each bag? Express your answer as a decimal correct to 2 decimal places.

4 A water bill showed that 7700 ℓ of water was used in a household of 8 adults in a week. If each member of the family used the same amount of water each day, how many litres of water were used by each person in a day?

5 Sharon puts an empty container under a leaking tap. In the first hour, $\frac{3}{8}\,\ell$ of water is collected. In the second hour, $\frac{1}{6}\,\ell$ of water is collected. How much water is collected in the container in the two hours?

6 Jamie bought $\frac{8}{9}\,$kg of minced meat. He used $\frac{3}{4}\,$kg of the minced meat to make some meatballs. How many kilograms of minced meat was left?

7. A snail was at the bottom of a well. In the first 10 minutes, the snail climbed $2\frac{7}{12}$ m. In the next 10 minutes, it climbed $1\frac{5}{7}$ m. How far was the snail from the bottom of the well after 20 minutes?

8. John is jogging along a track. He has already jogged $5\frac{2}{3}$ km. How many more kilometres does he have to jog to complete the track of $9\frac{1}{4}$ km?

Practice 8 — Word problems (2)

Solve these word problems. Show your workings clearly.

1. Mrs Quick bought 1 ℓ of milk. Michael drank $\frac{2}{7}$ ℓ of it and Joel drank $\frac{1}{3}$ ℓ of it. How many litres of milk were left?

2. Suzanne and Imaan each bought 4 identical cakes. They cut the cakes into equal pieces. The pieces of cake were shared equally among 5 friends. How many cakes did each friend get?

3   May had 5 pieces of paper. She cut each piece into 3 identical rectangles.
    The rectangular pieces of paper were shared equally among 6 pupils.
    How many rectangular pieces of paper did each pupil get?

4   Joe bought a plot of land. He planted tomatoes on $\frac{5}{9}$ of the land and
    broad beans on $\frac{1}{12}$ of the land. He planted potatoes on the remaining
    plot of land. What fraction of the land was planted with potatoes?

5 A tin contains three types of biscuits. The mass of chocolate biscuits is $1\frac{2}{9}$ kg. The mass of ginger biscuits is $2\frac{5}{6}$ kg. The total mass of the three types of biscuits is 5 kg. What is the mass of shortbread biscuits?

6 Bella and Victor go for a walk every morning. Bella walks $2\frac{1}{6}$ km. Victor walks $1\frac{3}{8}$ km less than Bella. What is the total distance they walk every morning?

7 🖩 Alice uses $\frac{3}{4}\ell$ of paint to colour her drawing. Belinda uses $\frac{4}{5}\ell$ more than Alice to colour her drawing. How many litres of paint do they use altogether?

8 🖩 A squirrel climbs $3\frac{3}{5}$ m up a tree 10 m high. It rests for a while and continues to climb another $4\frac{2}{3}$ m up the tree. How many more metres must the squirrel climb to reach the top of the tree?

Maths Journal

1 Tai found the answer to the following without using a calculator.

$$\frac{1}{8} + \frac{2}{3} = ?$$

Explain the steps used to add $\frac{1}{8}$ and $\frac{2}{3}$. Then work out the correct answer. You may use drawings to show how to work it out.

Challenging Practice

1 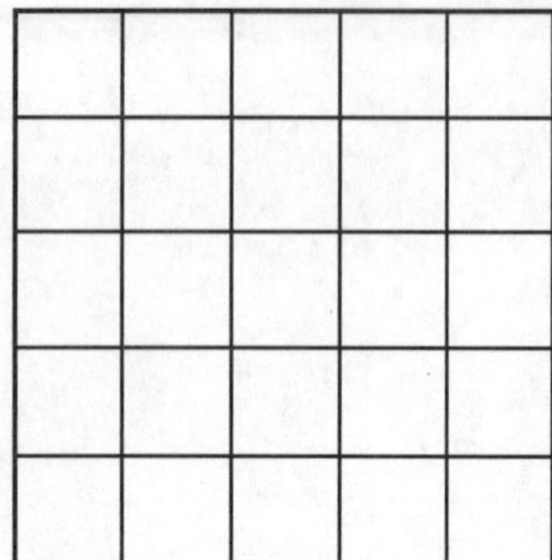 Ruby, Miya and Jack had a total of 25 similar square tiles to place over a square grid. Ruby used $\frac{8}{25}$ of the square tiles. Miya used $\frac{1}{5}$ of the square tiles. Shade the 5 × 5 square grid below to show how Ruby and Miya could have placed the square tiles. What fraction of the square grid must Jack place the tiles on so that $\frac{1}{5}$ of the square grid is **not** covered?

Fractions (2)

Date: ______________________

Practice 1 **Product of proper fractions**

1 Look at the diagram. Then fill in the spaces.

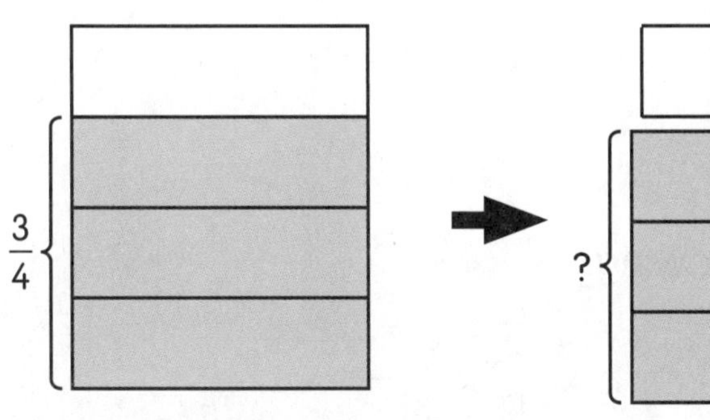

$$\frac{1}{2} \text{ of } \frac{3}{4} = \frac{\Box}{\Box} \times \frac{\Box}{\Box}$$

$$= \frac{\Box}{\Box}$$

2 Find the value of each of the following:

a $\quad \dfrac{1}{3} \text{ of } \dfrac{5}{8} = \dfrac{\Box}{\Box} \times \dfrac{\Box}{\Box}$

$$= \frac{\Box}{\Box}$$

b $\quad \dfrac{2}{7} \text{ of } \dfrac{9}{11} = \dfrac{\Box}{\Box} \times \dfrac{\Box}{\Box}$

$$= \frac{\Box}{\Box}$$

3 Find the value of each of the following. Express your answer in its simplest form.

a $\dfrac{2}{5}$ of $\dfrac{7}{10} = \dfrac{\square}{\square} \times \dfrac{\square}{\square}$

            $= \dfrac{\square}{\square}$

b $\dfrac{3}{4}$ of $\dfrac{8}{9} = \dfrac{\square}{\square} \times \dfrac{\square}{\square}$

            $= \dfrac{\square}{\square}$

4 Find the value of each of the following:

a $\dfrac{3}{8} \times \dfrac{1}{2} =$

b $\dfrac{5}{12} \times \dfrac{7}{8} =$

5 Find the value of each of the following:

a $\dfrac{2}{11} \times \dfrac{7}{12} =$

b $\dfrac{3}{8} \times \dfrac{4}{9} =$

Practice 2   Word problems (I)

Solve these word problems. Show your workings clearly.

1. Susie finished a job in $\frac{3}{4}$h. Megan finished it in $\frac{4}{5}$ of the time Susie took. How long did Megan take to finish the job?

2. Ben had a bottle containing $\frac{7}{8}\ell$ of milk. He poured $\frac{4}{5}$ of it into a bowl. What volume of milk did he pour into the bowl?

3. Anna ran $\frac{3}{4}$km in a race. Jess ran $\frac{2}{9}$ of the distance that Anna had run. What was the distance that Jess ran?

Solve these word problems. Show your workings clearly. Draw models to help you where necessary.

4 Meena bought some pieces of fruit. $\frac{4}{5}$ of her pieces of fruit were apples. $\frac{1}{2}$ of the apples she bought were red. What fraction of the pieces of fruit were red apples?

5 Richard worked in a factory packing computers. He packed $\frac{1}{3}$ of all the computers in the morning. $\frac{1}{2}$ of the computers he packed were shipped out immediately after packing. What fraction of all the computers in the factory was shipped out after packing?

    Unit 4: Fractions (2)

6 Mrs Mackay had some eggs in a basket. She took out $\frac{3}{5}$ of the eggs to bake some muffins and egg tarts. She used $\frac{2}{3}$ of the eggs taken out to bake muffins. What fraction of the total number of eggs was used to bake muffins?

7 Hardeep bought $\frac{5}{8}$ kg of tomatoes to make a salad. $\frac{2}{5}$ of the tomatoes were rotten and the rest were fresh. What was the mass of fresh tomatoes?

8 Jenny gave $\frac{1}{6}$ of her pocket money to her brother and spent $\frac{2}{5}$ of her remaining pocket money. What fraction of her total pocket money did she spend?

9 In a class, $\frac{3}{4}$ of the pupils liked football. $\frac{1}{3}$ of the pupils who did not like football were boys. What fraction of all the pupils were boys who did not like football?

Solve these word problems. Show your workings clearly. You may use your calculator where necessary.

10 Sonia had shells of three different sizes. $\frac{4}{9}$ of the shells were big and $\frac{2}{5}$ of the remainder were medium-sized. The rest of the shells were small. What fraction of the shells were small?

11 Millie made some origami animals. $\frac{5}{8}$ of them were birds and $\frac{1}{6}$ of the remainder were frogs. The rest were grasshoppers. What fraction of the origami animals were grasshoppers?

12 $\frac{2}{3}$ of the flowers in a garden were roses. $\frac{5}{12}$ of the roses were yellow and the rest were red. What fraction of the flowers were red?

13 Karen has a pile of coins. $\frac{1}{4}$ of her coins are European coins. $\frac{2}{9}$ of the European coins are euros. What fraction of her coins are not euros?

Practice 3   Product of an improper fraction and a proper or improper fraction

1 Look at the diagram. Then fill in the boxes.

a

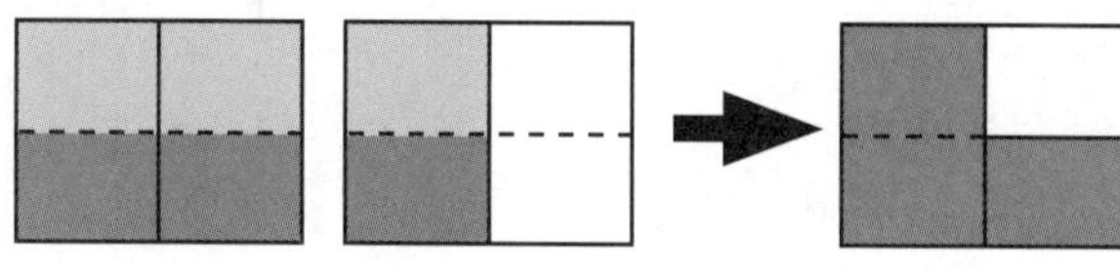

$$\frac{3}{2} \times \frac{1}{2} = \frac{\boxed{}}{\boxed{}}$$

b

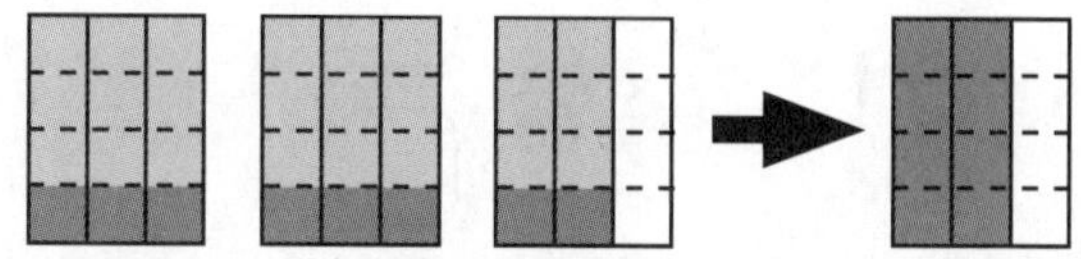

$$\frac{8}{3} \times \frac{1}{4} = \frac{\boxed{}}{\boxed{}}$$

2 Find the product.

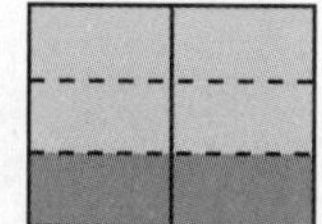 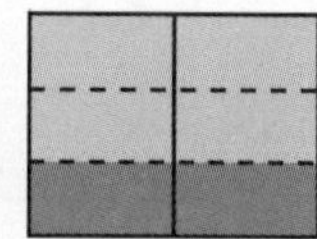 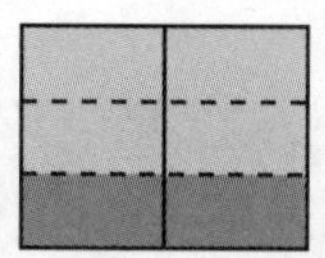 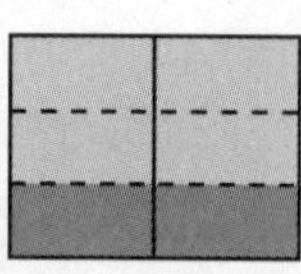 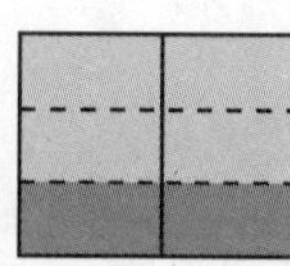 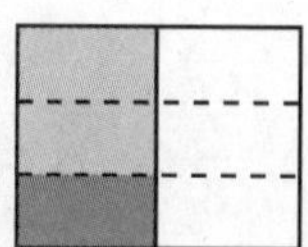
$$\frac{11}{2} \times \frac{1}{3}$$

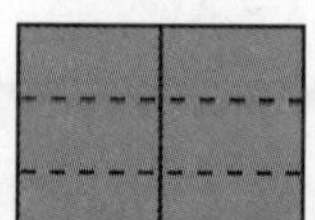 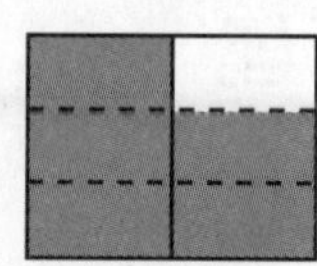 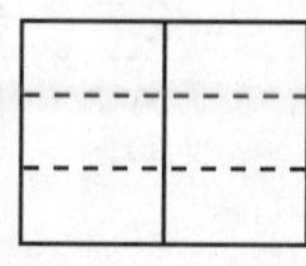 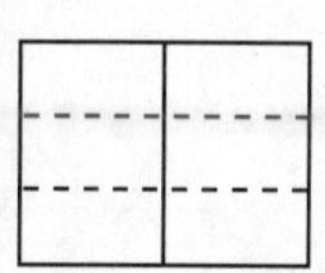 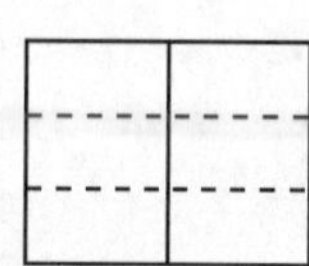 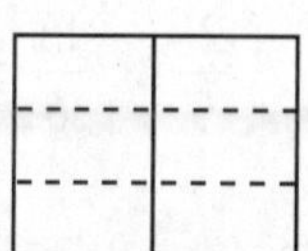

$$\frac{11}{2} \times \frac{1}{3} = \boxed{}\,\frac{\boxed{}}{\boxed{}}$$

3 Find the product of the fractions. Express your answer in its simplest form.

a $\dfrac{8}{3} \times \dfrac{3}{10} = \dfrac{\square}{\square}$

b $\dfrac{15}{9} \times \dfrac{3}{20} = \dfrac{\square}{\square}$

c $\dfrac{2}{5} \times \dfrac{15}{4} = \square\dfrac{\square}{\square}$

d $\dfrac{16}{7} \times \dfrac{21}{2} = \square$

e $\dfrac{7}{4} \times \dfrac{1}{3} = \dfrac{\square}{\square}$

f $\dfrac{9}{8} \times \dfrac{2}{7} = \dfrac{\square}{\square}$

4 Find the product of the fractions.

a $\dfrac{15}{12} \times \dfrac{5}{8} = $ _______

b $\dfrac{32}{9} \times \dfrac{36}{8} = $ _______

c $\dfrac{7}{8} \times \dfrac{6}{5} = $ _______

d $\dfrac{11}{12} \times \dfrac{28}{3} = $ _______

e $\dfrac{21}{5} \times \dfrac{15}{6} = $ _______

f $\dfrac{25}{4} \times \dfrac{18}{10} = $ _______

g $\dfrac{30}{9} \times \dfrac{7}{2} = $ _______

h $\dfrac{14}{8} \times \dfrac{5}{3} = $ _______

Practice 4 — Product of a mixed number and a whole number

1. Look at the diagram. Then fill in the boxes.

a

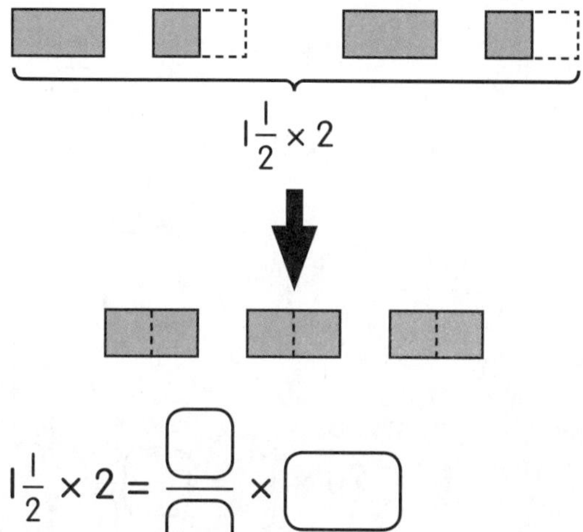

$$1\frac{1}{2} \times 2$$

$$1\frac{1}{2} \times 2 = \frac{\boxed{}}{\boxed{}} \times \boxed{}$$

$$= \boxed{}$$

b

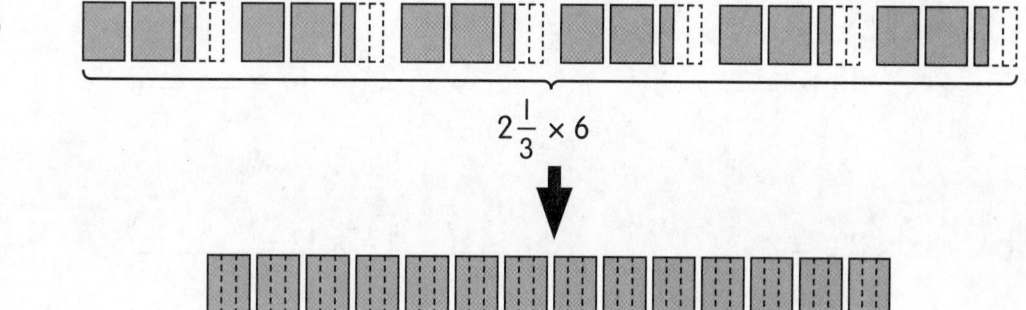

$$2\frac{1}{3} \times 6$$

$$2\frac{1}{3} \times 6 = \frac{\boxed{}}{\boxed{}} \times \boxed{}$$

$$= \boxed{}$$

2 ⌨ Find the product.

a $4\frac{1}{5} \times 15 =$ ☐

b $2\frac{3}{7} \times 28 =$ ☐

c $24 \times 1\frac{5}{6} =$ ☐

d $21 \times 2\frac{5}{9} =$ ☐

e $14 \times 2\frac{7}{9} =$ ☐

f $26 \times 1\frac{1}{6} =$ ☐

3 ⌨ Find the product.

a $4\frac{1}{2} \times 18 =$ _____

b $2\frac{3}{4} \times 16 =$ _____

c $32 \times 3\frac{1}{8} =$ _____

d $1\frac{4}{5} \times 12 =$ _____

e $15 \times 2\frac{3}{7} =$ _____

f $12 \times 2\frac{3}{8} =$ _____

g $9 \times 2\frac{1}{3} =$ _____

h $7 \times 2\frac{1}{4} =$ _____

Practice 5 — Word problems (2)

Solve these word problems. You may use your calculator in this section.

1 At a party, there were 8 guests. Each guest ate $2\frac{1}{4}$ oranges. How many oranges did the 8 guests eat in total?

I guest $\longrightarrow$ $2\frac{1}{4}$ oranges

8 guests $\longrightarrow$ _______ × _______

= _______ oranges

2 One kilogram of chicken cost £3. Tim bought $8\frac{2}{3}$ kg of chicken. How much did Tim pay for the chicken?

3 Omar tied up a parcel with $2\frac{1}{4}$ m of string. He tied up a total of 20 of these parcels. How many metres of string did he use?

4 The length of a picture is 2 m and its width is $1\frac{2}{5}$ m. Find the area of the picture. Express your answer as a decimal.

5 Jacob bought 5 pieces of material to make pillowcases. Each piece of material was $1\frac{7}{8}$ m long.

    a What was the total length of material he bought?

    b One metre of the material cost £6. How much did he pay for all the material?

6 Mrs Kent's family eats $12\frac{3}{4}$ kg of potatoes a month. The cost of 1 kg of potatoes is £2. Find the cost of the potatoes her family eats in a year.

Practice 6   Dividing a fraction by a whole number

1 Shade parts of the model to show the division. Then fill in the answers.

a $\frac{1}{3} \div 2$

$\frac{\boxed{}}{\boxed{}}$ is shaded.

$\frac{1}{3} \div 2 =$ _______

b $\frac{1}{6} \div 3$

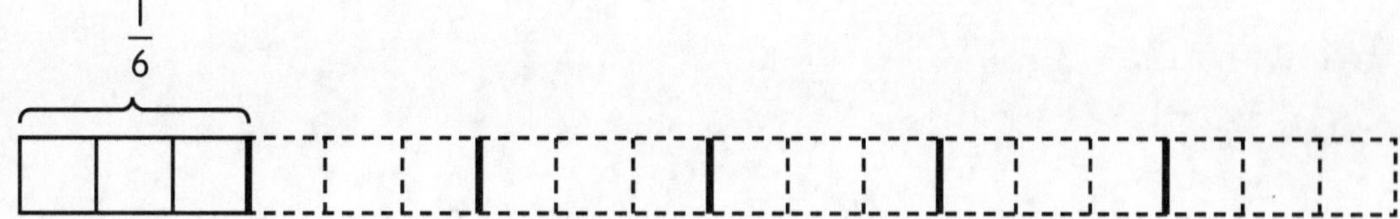

$\frac{\boxed{}}{\boxed{}}$ is shaded.

$\frac{1}{6} \div 3 =$ _______

2 Divide. Draw models to help you where necessary.

a $\dfrac{4}{5} \div 2 =$ **b** $\dfrac{6}{7} \div 3 =$

c $\dfrac{3}{4} \div 2 =$ **d** $\dfrac{2}{5} \div 3 =$

3 Divide. Express your answer in its simplest form.

a $\dfrac{4}{5} \div 7 =$ **b** $\dfrac{5}{8} \div 9 =$

c $\dfrac{8}{9} \div 4 =$ **d** $\dfrac{10}{11} \div 5 =$

Solve these word problems. Show your workings clearly.

4 Mr Green had $\frac{2}{5}$ of a cake. He divided the cake equally among 4 pupils. What fraction of the cake did each pupil get?

5 Jake pours $\frac{4}{9}\ell$ of milk from a jug equally into 4 cups. Find the amount of milk, in litres:

a in each cup?

b in 3 cups?

6 Max bought $\frac{3}{5}$ kg of pumpkin. He divided the pumpkin into 6 equal portions.

a Find the mass, in kilograms, of 1 portion of pumpkin.

b Find the total mass, in kilograms, of 4 portions of pumpkin.

7 Alicia bought a plot of land with an area of $\frac{2}{5}$ km². She divided the land equally into 8 small plots. What was the total area of 3 of the small plots of land?

Practice 7 — Word problems (3)

Solve these word problems. Show your workings clearly. Draw models to help you where necessary.

1. Liam writes 72 pages of a story in a day. He writes $\frac{1}{2}$ of the pages in the morning and $\frac{1}{3}$ of the pages in the afternoon. He writes the rest of the pages in the evening. How many pages of the story does he write altogether in the morning and afternoon?

2. Last Saturday, Ravi spent 6 hours altogether reading, playing games and chatting with his friends. He spent $\frac{2}{5}$ of the time reading and $\frac{1}{2}$ of the time playing games. How many minutes did he spend chatting with his friends?

3 Abby's dad earns £720 a week. He spends $\frac{1}{3}$ of his money on rent and $\frac{3}{4}$ of the remaining money on shopping. How much money does he spend on both rent and shopping?

4 A box contained pieces of fruit such as apples, oranges and pears. $\frac{3}{5}$ of the pieces of fruit were apples. $\frac{1}{4}$ of the remaining pieces of fruit were oranges and the rest were pears. If there were 60 pears in the box, how many oranges were there?

Unit 4: Fractions (2)

5 Sian opened a 2 kg packet of flour. She used $\frac{4}{9}$ of the flour to make a pizza. Then she used $\frac{2}{7}$ of the remaining flour to make bread. Find the mass of the packet of flour that she had left.
Give your answer to 2 decimal places.

6 During a triathlon, Sharon swam $\frac{1}{4}$ of the total route and cycled $\frac{3}{5}$ of the remaining route. She jogged the rest of the route. If she jogged 3600 m, find the total distance of the route.

Maths Journal

1. Ella solved the following word problem in 2 ways.

> Eddie ate $\frac{1}{2}$ of a pie. Rob ate $\frac{1}{2}$ of the remainder.
> What fraction of the pie was left?

Show 2 different ways of solving the word problem. You may draw a model if necessary.

Challenging Practice

1. Fill in the spaces.

   a $\dfrac{2}{3} + \dfrac{2}{3} + \dfrac{2}{3} + \dfrac{2}{3} + \dfrac{2}{3} =$ _____ $\times \dfrac{2}{3}$

   b $\dfrac{1}{4} + \dfrac{1}{4} + \dfrac{1}{4} + \dfrac{1}{8} + \dfrac{1}{8} =$ _____ $\times \dfrac{1}{4}$

2. Lisa was given half of a cake and Nick was given $\dfrac{1}{3}$ of the other half. The remaining cake was shared equally among 8 pupils. What fraction of the whole cake did each of the 8 pupils get?

Problem Solving

1. Jim and Sheena each had an identical cottage pie. Jim ate $\frac{2}{3}$ of his cottage pie and Sheena ate $\frac{1}{4}$ of her cottage pie. Jim ate 150 g more cottage pie than Sheena. What was the mass of each cottage pie?

2. Mr Clark had some pineapples for sale. He sold 24 pineapples in the morning. In the afternoon, he sold $\frac{2}{7}$ of the remainder. Then he had $\frac{1}{2}$ of the total number of pineapples left. How many pineapples did Mr Clark have at first?

Review 2

1 Express each fraction in its simplest form.

    a $\dfrac{6}{14}$ = _______   **b** $\dfrac{9}{24}$ = _______

    c $\dfrac{5}{10}$ = _______   **d** $\dfrac{15}{18}$ = _______

2 For each pair of fractions, find the lowest common multiple of the denominators. Then express both fractions with the same denominator.

    a $\dfrac{2}{3}, \dfrac{7}{12}$ **b** $\dfrac{1}{3}, \dfrac{5}{8}$

   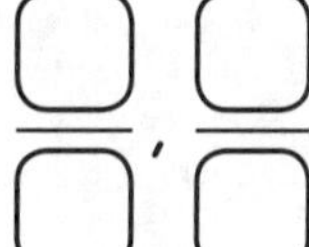

3 Shade to find the sum of $\dfrac{1}{3}$ and $\dfrac{3}{5}$ on the model. Then complete the addition sentence.

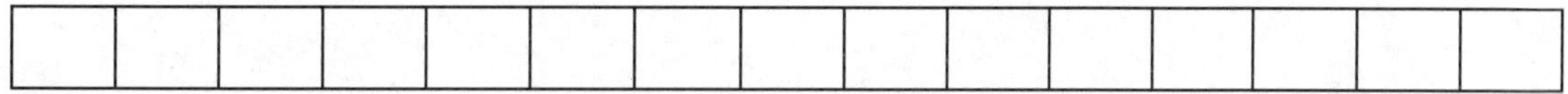

    $\dfrac{1}{3} + \dfrac{3}{5}$ = _______ + _______

               = _______

4 Add. Express your answer in its simplest form where necessary.

   a $\dfrac{3}{4} + \dfrac{1}{12} =$ **b** $\dfrac{3}{5} + \dfrac{2}{7} =$

5 Shade to find the difference of $\dfrac{4}{5}$ and $\dfrac{2}{3}$ on the model. Then complete the subtraction sentence.

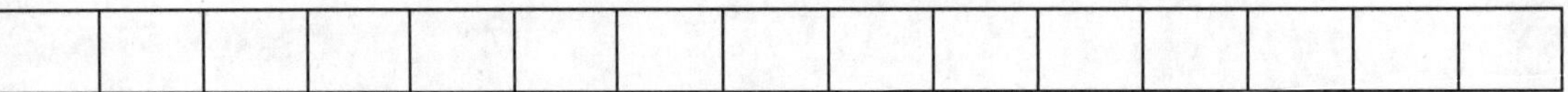

$$\dfrac{4}{5} - \dfrac{2}{3} = \underline{\hspace{3em}} - \underline{\hspace{3em}}$$

$$= \underline{\hspace{3em}}$$

6 Subtract. Express your answer in its simplest form where necessary.

   a $\dfrac{3}{4} - \dfrac{1}{12} =$ **b** $\dfrac{3}{5} - \dfrac{3}{9} =$

7 Write each division sentence as a fraction.

   a $4 \div 9 = \dfrac{\Box}{\Box}$ **b** $4 \div 11 = \dfrac{\Box}{\Box}$

8 Write each fraction as a division sentence.

a $\dfrac{5}{6} = $ _______ $\div$ _______   **b** $\dfrac{7}{12} = $ _______ $\div$ _______

9 Express each fraction as a decimal. Round your answer to 2 decimal places where necessary.

a $\dfrac{4}{5} = $ _______   **b** $\dfrac{2}{9} \approx $ _______   **c** $\dfrac{5}{12} \approx $ _______

10 Divide. Express your answer as a mixed number. Where necessary, express your answer in its simplest form.

a $7 \div 5 =$ **b** $19 \div 4 =$

c $22 \div 8 =$ **d** $28 \div 6 =$

11 Express each division sentence as a mixed number and as a decimal correct to 2 decimal places where necessary.

Division Sentence		Division Sentence Expressed as:	
		a Mixed Number	a Decimal
a	$8 \div 3$		
b	$13 \div 4$		
c	$18 \div 7$		
d	$23 \div 5$		

Solve these word problems. Show your workings clearly.

12 Ron used $\frac{3}{5}$ kg of flour to make bread and $\frac{2}{7}$ kg of flour to make scones. How many more kilograms of flour did he use to make bread than scones?

13 Henry cycled $2\frac{1}{4}$ km to the park to meet his friend. Then he cycled $1\frac{2}{5}$ km to the sandwich shop to get some lunch. What was the total distance Henry cycled?

14 Tina used $4\frac{5}{12}$ m of thread to sew a costume. Kelvin used $1\frac{2}{3}$ m of thread to mend his shirt. How many metres of thread did they use altogether?

15 Tom and Aisha had an equal number of eggs at first. Then Tom sold $\frac{1}{3}$ of his eggs and Aisha sold $\frac{3}{4}$ of her eggs. If Aisha sold 250 more eggs than Tom, how many eggs did each person have at first?

16 Ros poured $1\frac{3}{4}\ell$ of orange juice into a container. She added $3\frac{1}{3}\ell$ of mango juice into the container. She then poured $2\frac{2}{3}\ell$ of the mixed juice into a jug. How many litres of mixed juice were left in the container?

17 Find the value of:

a $\quad \dfrac{2}{5}$ of $\dfrac{10}{11} =$

b $\quad \dfrac{8}{9}$ of $\dfrac{5}{12} =$

c $\quad \dfrac{6}{7} \times \dfrac{5}{8} =$

d $\quad \dfrac{4}{5} \times \dfrac{10}{12} =$

18 Find the product.

a $\quad \dfrac{2}{5} \times \dfrac{15}{7} =$

b $\quad \dfrac{9}{5} \times \dfrac{5}{12} =$

c $\quad \dfrac{4}{3} \times \dfrac{7}{6} =$

d $\quad \dfrac{8}{3} \times \dfrac{9}{12} =$

19 Find the product.

a $\quad 2\dfrac{1}{4} \times 16 =$

b $\quad 27 \times 1\dfrac{2}{9} =$

c $\quad 5\dfrac{3}{6} \times 42 =$

d $\quad 55 \times 6\dfrac{3}{11} =$

e $\quad 2\dfrac{5}{6} \times 15 =$

f $\quad 45 \times 2\dfrac{5}{12} =$

20 Divide. Express your answer in its simplest form.

a $\dfrac{7}{8} \div 5 =$ **b** $\dfrac{9}{11} \div 4 =$

c $\dfrac{4}{7} \div 12 =$ **d** $\dfrac{3}{7} \div 6 =$

e $\dfrac{5}{8} \div 4 =$ **f** $\dfrac{2}{9} \div 6 =$

Solve these word problems. Show your workings clearly.

21 Matt bought $\dfrac{8}{9}$ kg of chicken. He used $\dfrac{1}{4}$ of it to make chicken soup. How many kilograms of chicken did he use to make the soup?

22 In a race, Joshua covered a total distance of $\frac{11}{12}$ km. He ran $\frac{4}{5}$ of the distance and walked the rest of the way. How many kilometres did he run?

23 On a picnic, 12 children each got $3\frac{1}{4}$ sandwiches. How many sandwiches did the children get altogether?

24 Mr Ali used $4\frac{3}{8}$ kg of meat to prepare a pot of soup. He cooked 12 identical pots of soup. How many kilograms of meat did he use altogether?

25 Ella poured $\frac{3}{8}\ell$ of jelly mix equally into 9 jelly moulds. Find the volume of jelly mix in 2 of these moulds.

26 Sally sold 135 cabbages in a day. She sold $\frac{1}{3}$ of the cabbages in the first hour and $\frac{2}{5}$ of the cabbages in the second hour. How many cabbages did she sell altogether in the two hours?

27 $\frac{1}{7}$ of a school's garden was used to grow vegetables. $\frac{1}{3}$ of the remaining garden was used to grow flowers. What fraction of the garden was used to grow flowers?

28 Jan's family spent £840 on a holiday. They spent $\frac{2}{3}$ of the amount on the accommodation and $\frac{1}{2}$ of the remaining amount on food. How much did they spend on the accommodation and food altogether?

29 Matthew used $\frac{1}{5}$ of a box of sugar for biscuits and $\frac{3}{4}$ of the remainder to make bread. The rest of the sugar was packed equally into 5 packets. What fraction of the total amount of sugar was in each packet?

30 Saleem travelled $\frac{1}{4}$ of a journey by bus. He jogged $\frac{1}{2}$ of the remaining distance and walked the rest of the journey. If he walked 800 m, what was the total distance he travelled?

31 Serena's mum filled up $\frac{7}{8}$ of her petrol tank for a trip. She used $\frac{6}{11}$ of the petrol by the end of the trip. The capacity of her petrol tank was 70 ℓ. How much petrol did she use for the trip?

Express your answer as a decimal correct to 1 decimal place.

32 $\frac{3}{10}$ of the seats on a train were first class seats. The rest were standard seats. $\frac{4}{5}$ of the standard seats were occupied. What fraction of all seats were unoccupied standard seats?

33 Kerry had some boxes of vegetables for sale. She sold 35 boxes on Monday. She sold $\frac{1}{5}$ of the remaining boxes of vegetables on Tuesday. Then she had $\frac{1}{3}$ of the total number of boxes of vegetables left. How many boxes of vegetables did she have at first?

34 Alisha uses $\frac{1}{4}$ of a packet of flour to make bread. She uses $\frac{1}{9}$ of the remainder to make pizza. What fraction of the packet of flour does she have left?

35 300 people attended a party. After one hour, $\frac{1}{3}$ of the number of people left the party. After another hour, $\frac{3}{10}$ of the remaining people left the party. How many people were left at the party in the end?

Area of a Triangle

Practice 1 — Base and height of a triangle

1. In each triangle, a base or a height is given. Name the related height or base.

a

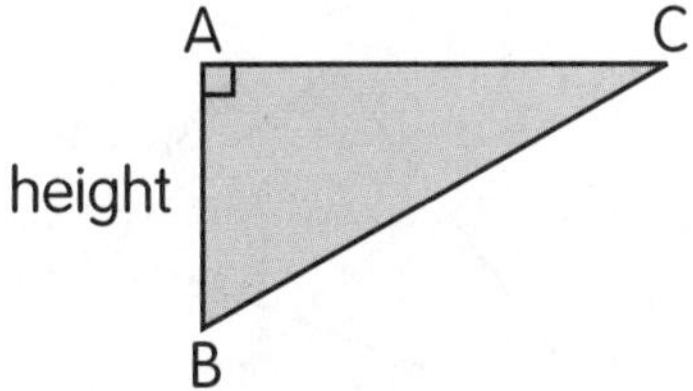

Base: _______________

b

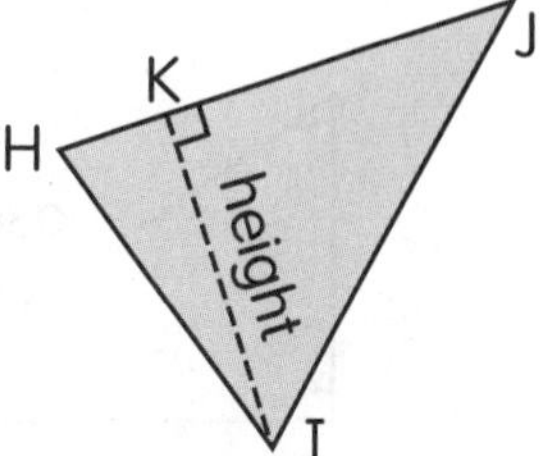

Base: _______________

c

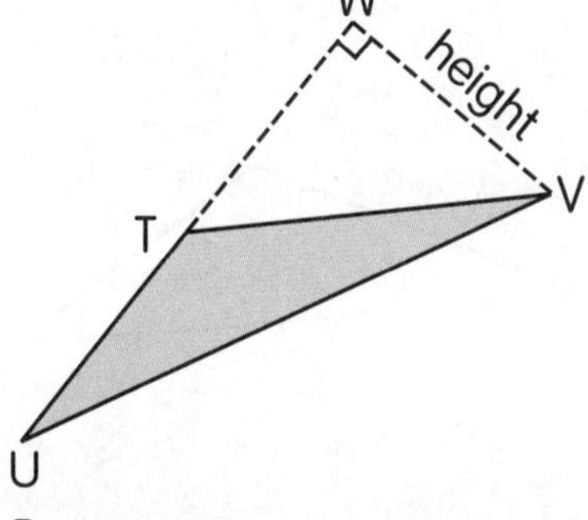

Base: _______________

d

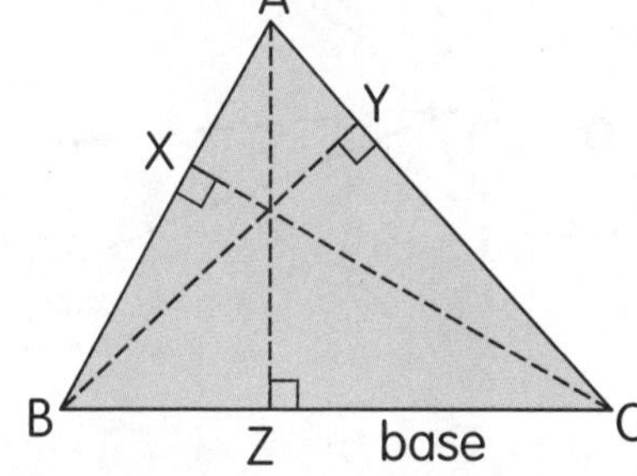

Height: _______________

e

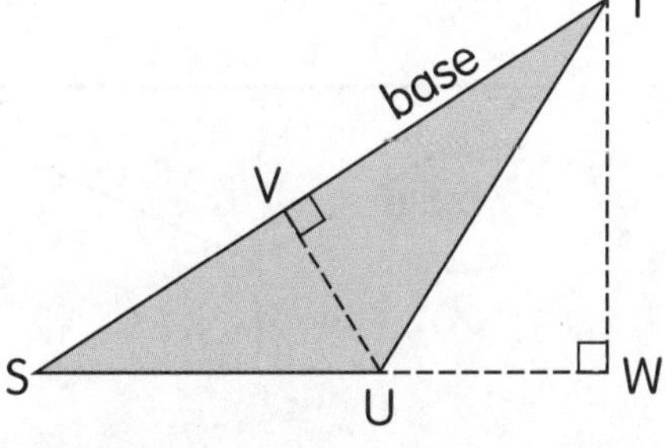

Height: _______________

f

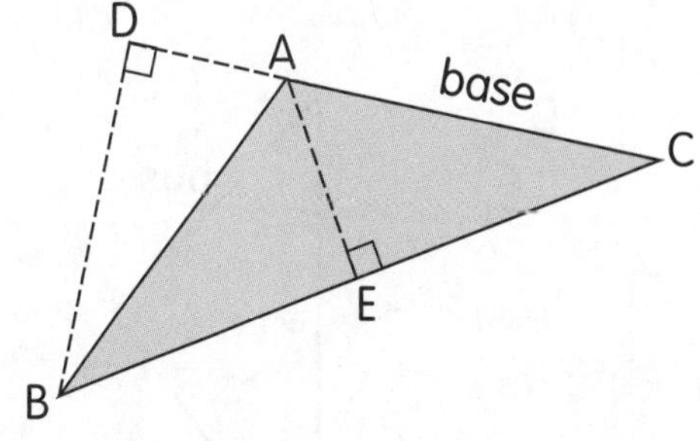

Height: _______________

 For each triangle, the base is given. Label the height. Use a set-square to draw the height where necessary.

a

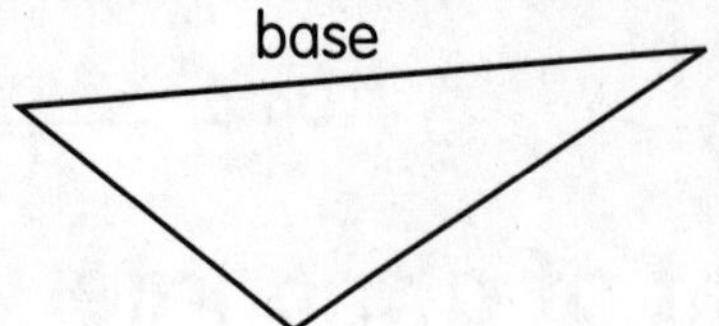

b

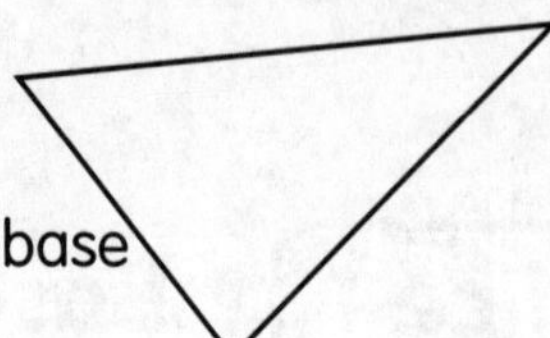

c

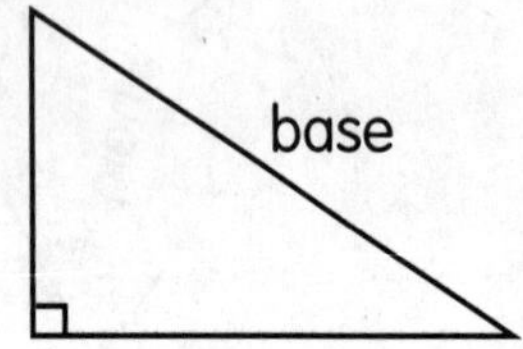

d

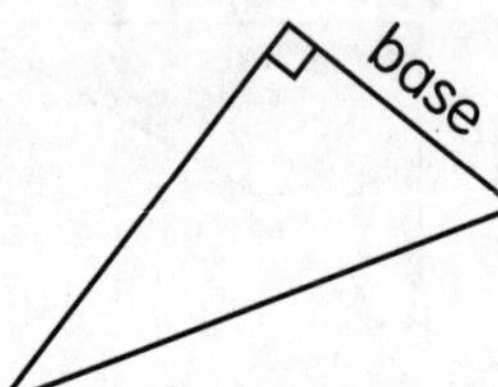

e

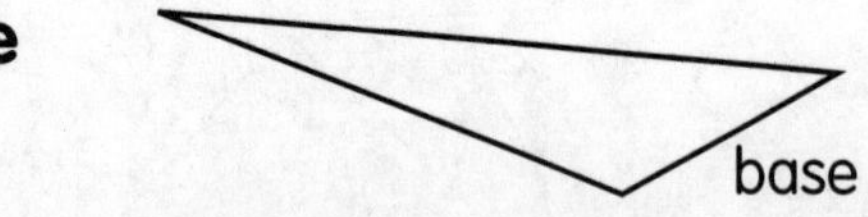

f

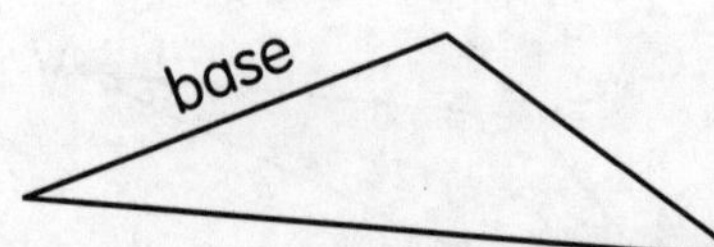

g

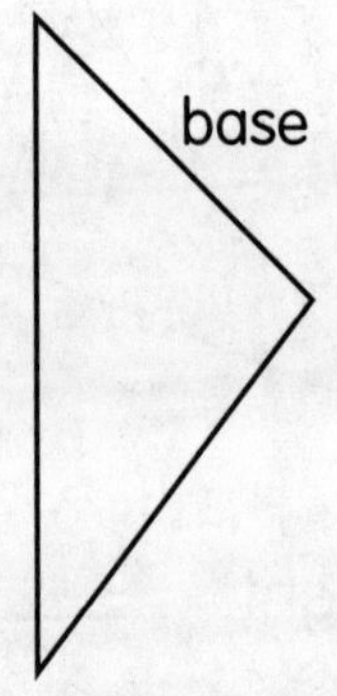

h

Practice 2   Finding the area of a triangle

1 Find the area of each shaded triangle. Write down each step and give your answers in the correct units.

a

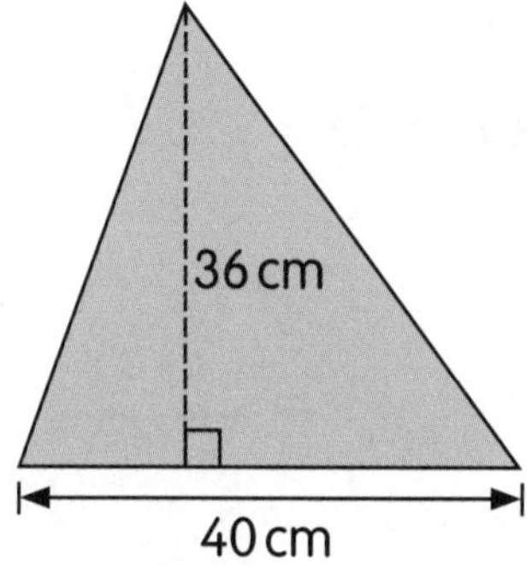

Area of triangle = $\frac{1}{2}$ × Base × Height

$= \dfrac{1}{2} \times 40 \times 36$

= _______________

= _______________

b

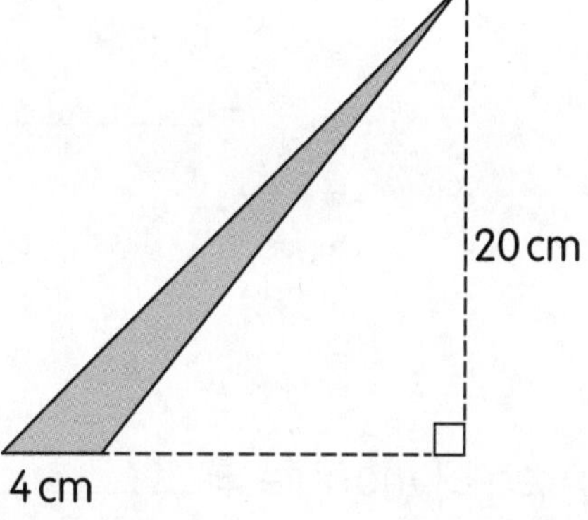

Area of triangle = _______________

= _______________

c

Area of triangle = _______________

= _______________

d

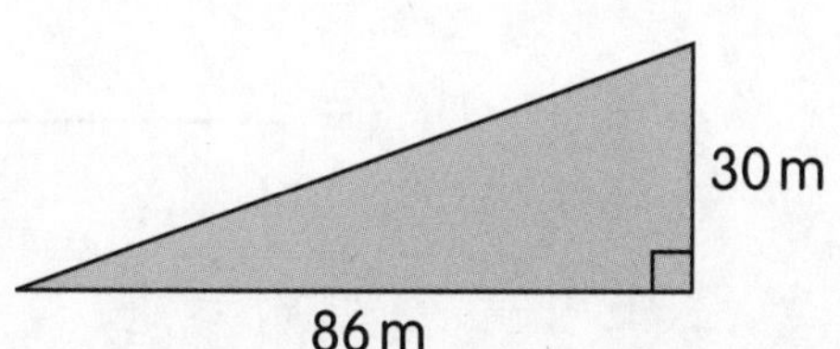

Area of triangle = _______________

= _______________

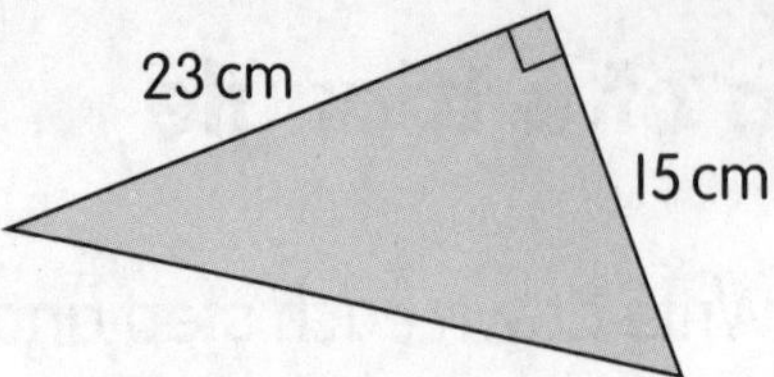

Area of triangle = _______________

= _______________

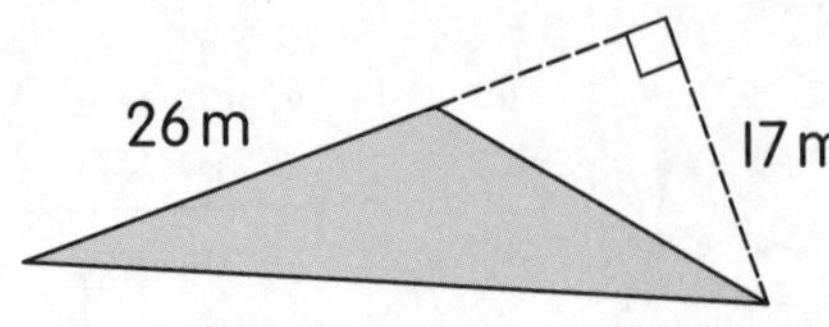

Area of triangle = _______________

= _______________

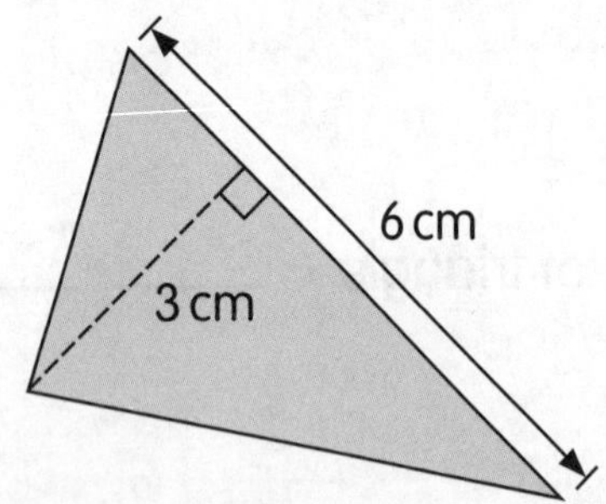

Area of triangle = _______________

= _______________

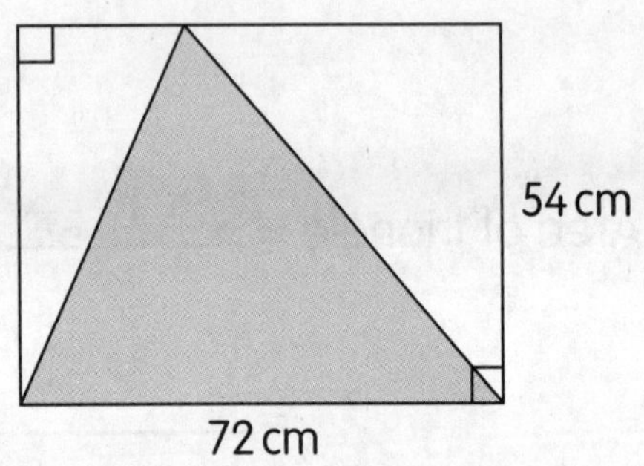

Area of triangle = _______________

= _______________

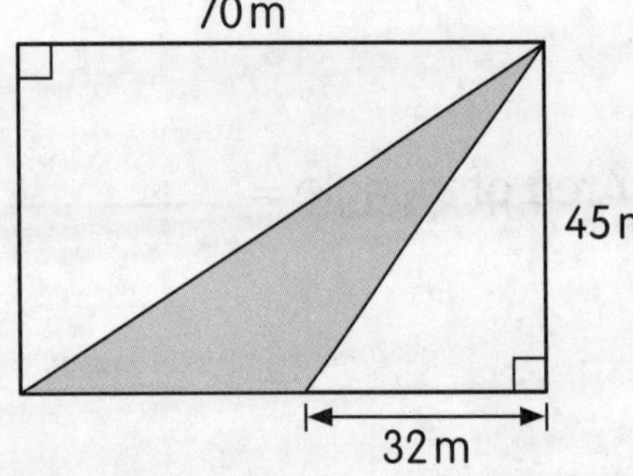

Area of triangle = _______________

= _______________

2 Find the area of each shaded triangle.

a

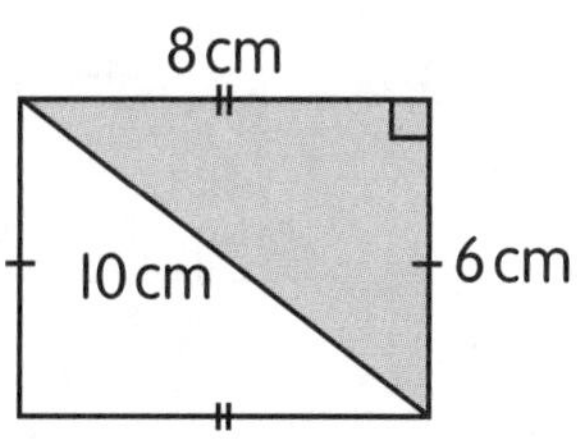

Area = $\frac{1}{2}$ × _______ × _______

= _______________

b

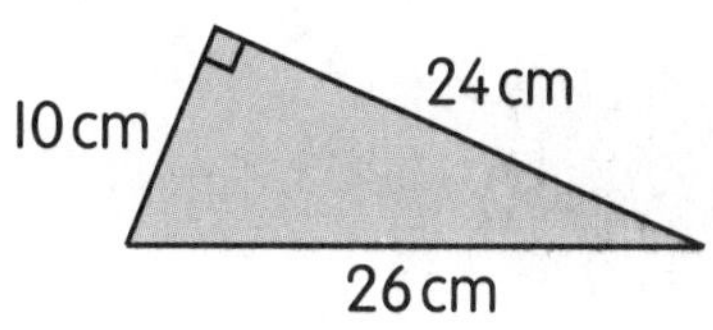

Area = _______________

c

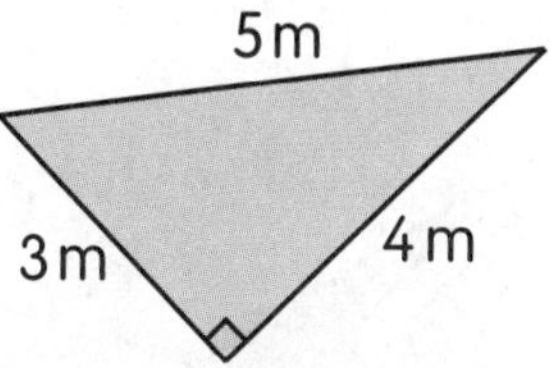

Area = _______________

d

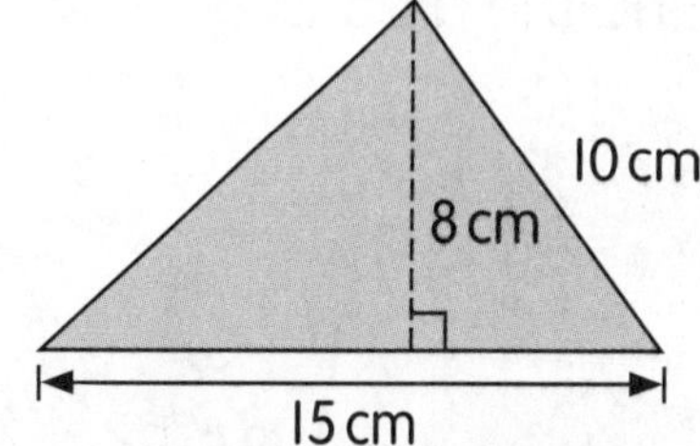

Area = _______________

3 Find the area of each shaded triangle.

a

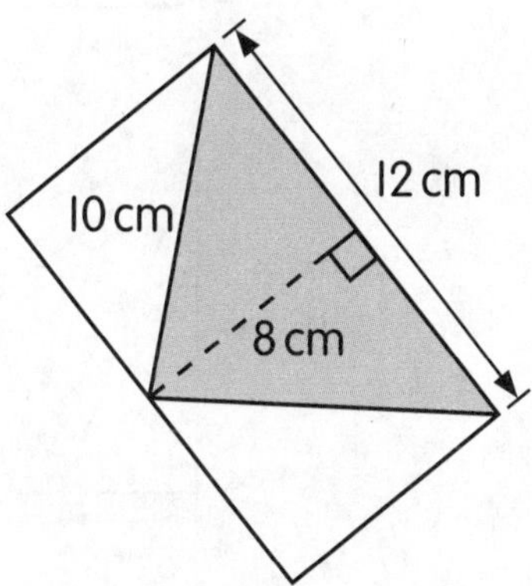

Area = $\frac{1}{2}$ × _______ × _______

= _______________

b

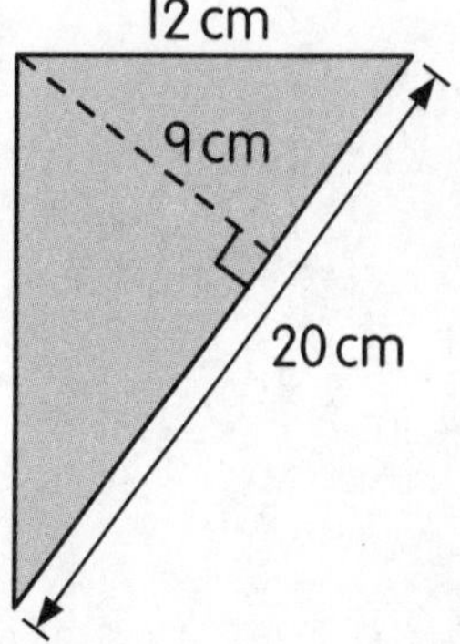

Area = _______________

c

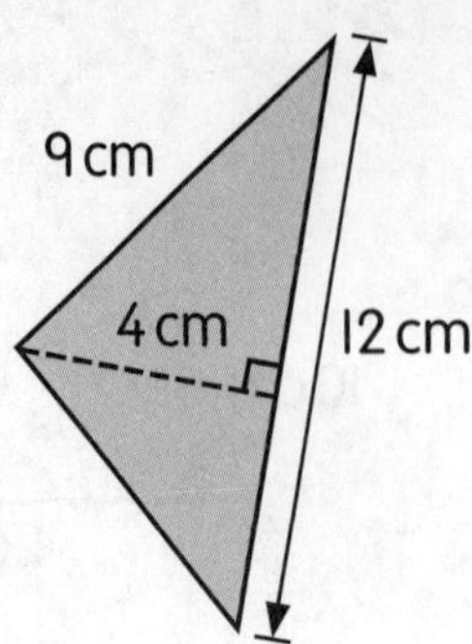

Area = ______________

d

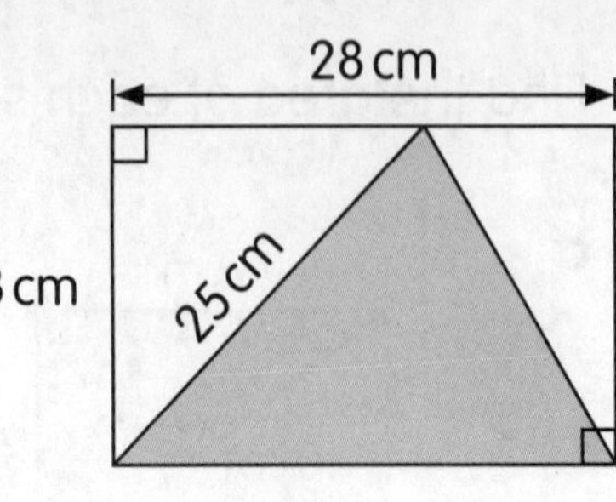

Area = ______________

---

4 Find the area of each shaded triangle.

a

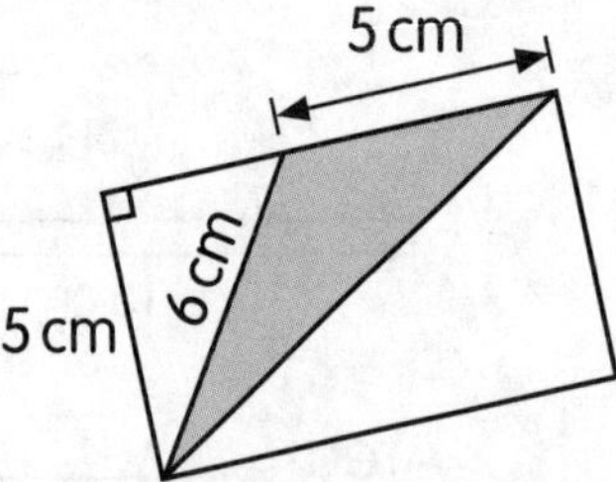

Area = $\frac{1}{2}$ × ______ × ______

= ______________

b

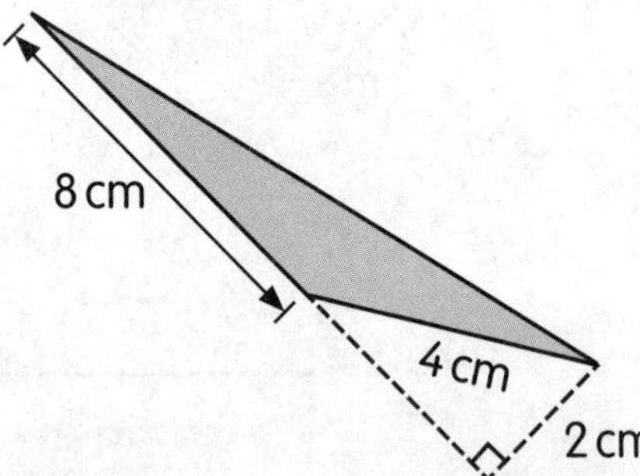

Area = ______________

c

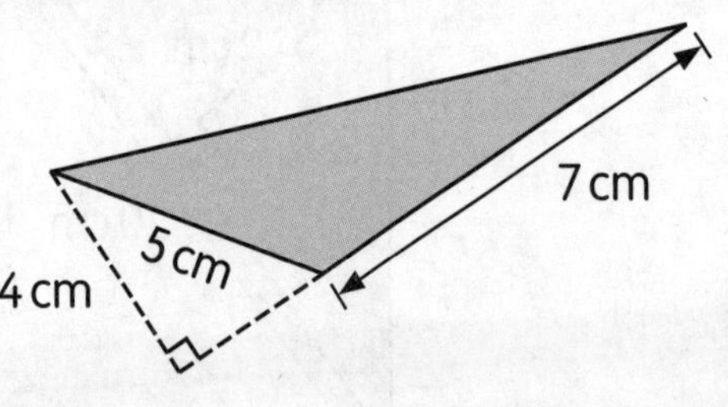

Area = ______________

d

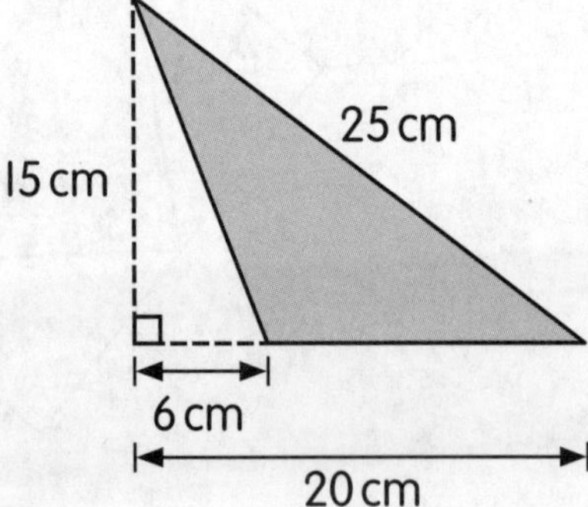

Area = ______________

Maths Journal

1 Four pupils worked out the area
of the shaded triangle on the right.

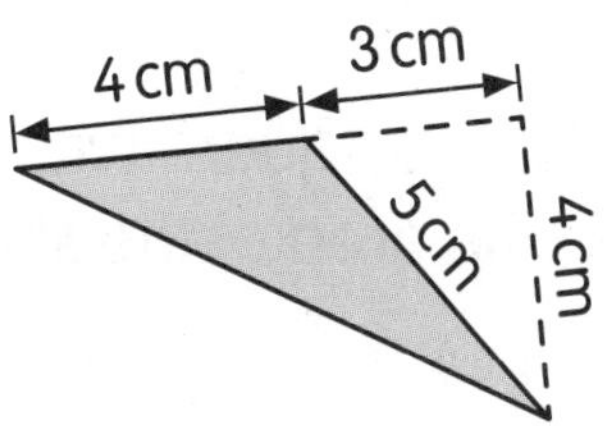

The following are their workings.

Zack: $4 \times 4 = 16\,cm^2$

Patrick: $\frac{1}{2} \times 5 \times 4 = 10\,cm^2$

Becky: $\frac{1}{2} \times 7 \times 4 = 14\,cm^2$

James: $\frac{1}{2} \times 3 \times 4 = 6\,cm^2$

Explain the mistakes they have made. Then write the correct answer.

Zack: ____

Patrick: ____

Becky: ____

James: ____

The area of the shaded triangle is: ______________________

2 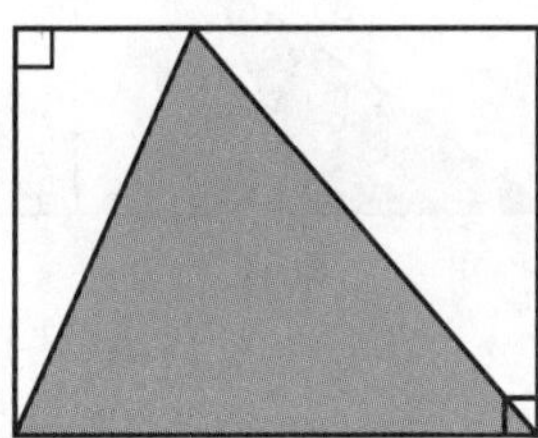 The area of the shaded triangle is $15\,cm^2$.
Explain why the area of the rectangle is $30\,cm^2$.

Challenging Practice

1 ABCD is a square with 10 cm sides and BE = EC.
Find the area of the shaded triangle.

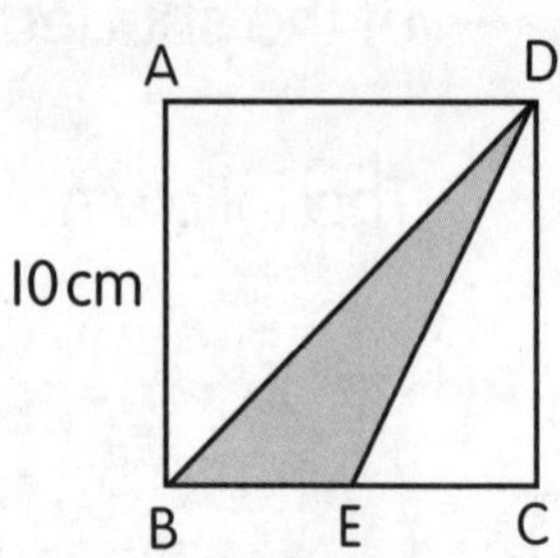

2 ABCD is a rectangle 18 cm by 8 cm.
AE = ED and AF = FB. Find the area of the
shaded triangle.

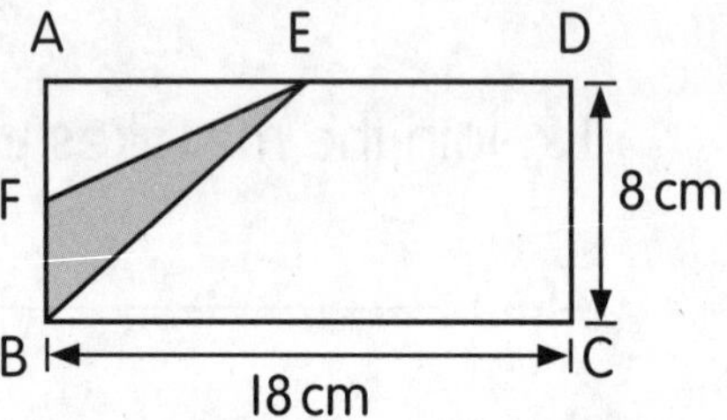

3 ABCD is a rectangle with an area of 48 cm².
The length of CD is 3 times the length of DF.
BC = 4 cm.

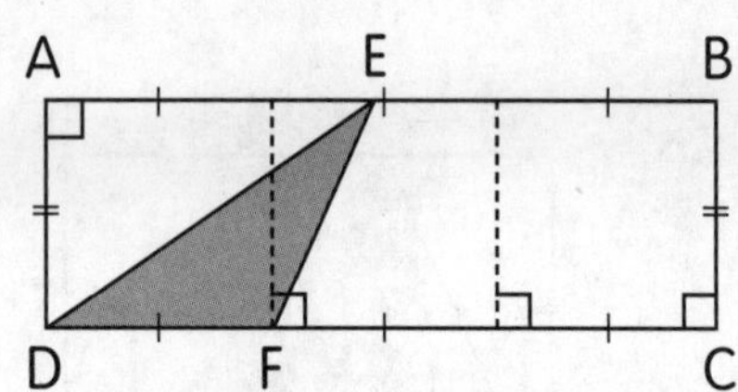

    a Find the length of the rectangle.
    b Find the area of the shaded triangle.

4 ABCD is a rectangle 12 cm by 5 cm.
BE = 4 cm. Find the area of the shaded region, ABED.

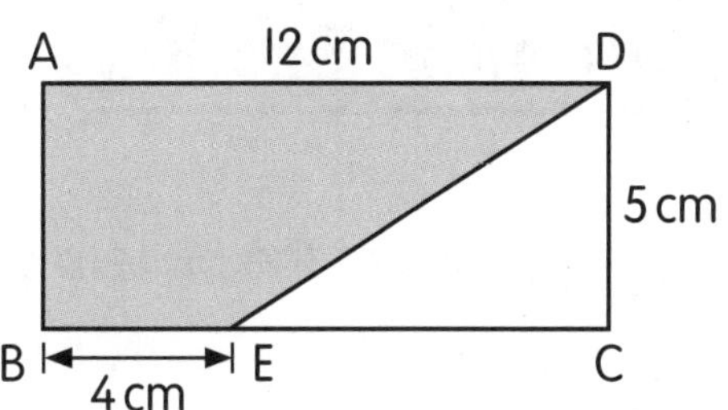

5 ABCD is a square with 8 cm sides.
AE = AF = 4 cm. Find the area of the shaded triangle, CEF.

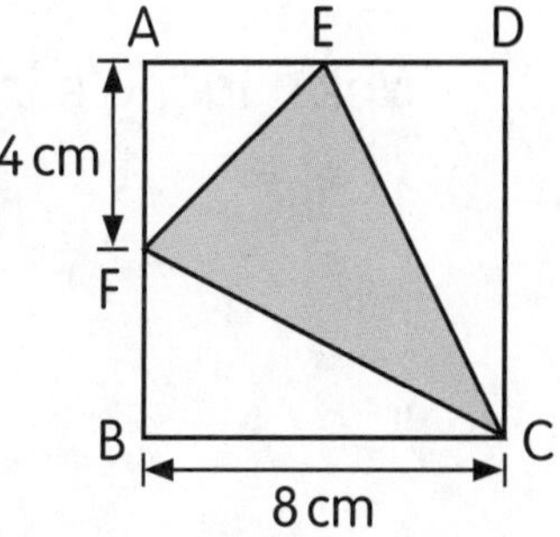

6 The perimeter of rectangle ABCD is 256 cm. Its length is 3 times as long as its width. Find the area of triangle ABC.

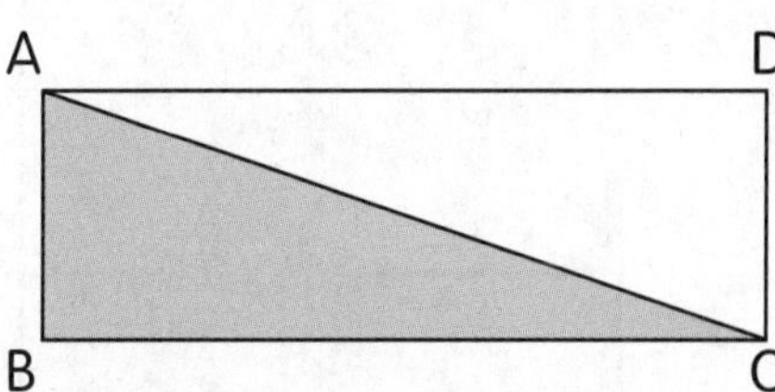

Problem Solving

1. 🖩 Look at the pattern of triangles below.

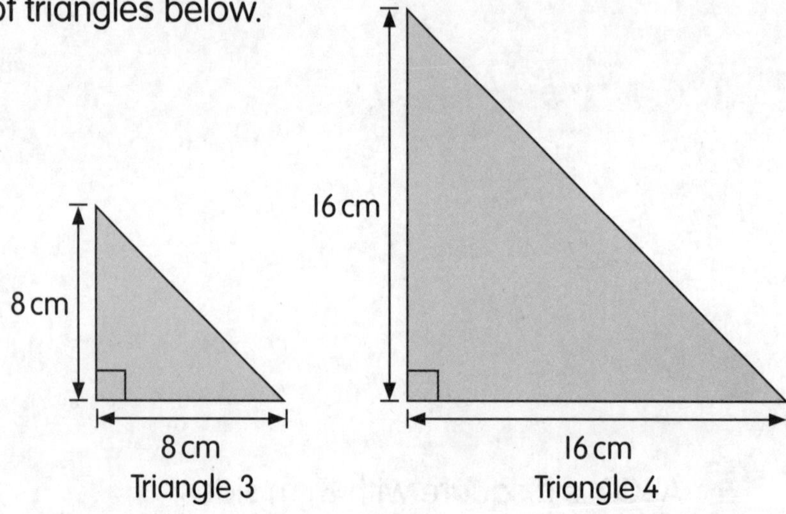

What is the area of Triangle 5 in the pattern? ________________

Which triangle in the pattern will have an area of 32 768 cm^2? ________________

2. ABCD is a square with 20 cm sides.
AX = XB, BY = YC, CZ = ZD, AW = WD. WY and XZ are straight lines.
Find the total area of the shaded parts.

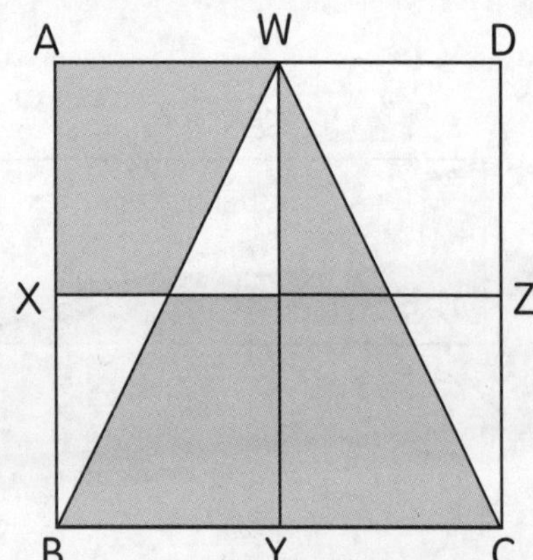

Ratio

Date: _______________

Practice 1   Finding ratio

1 The table below shows the number of football cards each child has.

a   Find the number of football cards they have altogether.

Child	Number of Football Cards
Farha	8
Peter	3
Jack	5
Omar	11
Total	

b   Fill in the table below to show the ratios.

The Ratio of ...	Ratio
the number of football cards Farha has to the number of football cards Omar has is	8 : 11
the number of football cards Jack has to the number of football cards Peter has is	
the number of football cards Peter has to the number of football cards Jack has is	
the number of football cards Farha has to the total number of football cards is	
the total number of football cards to the number of football cards Omar has is	

2   Mr Woods puts some pencils into bundles of 10. He gives Chantal 4 bundles and Lisa 9 bundles of pencils.

a   The ratio of the number of pencils Chantal has to the number of pencils Lisa has is _____ : _____ .

b   The ratio of the number of pencils Lisa has to the number of pencils Chantal has is _____ : _____ .

c   The ratio of the number of pencils Lisa has to the total number of pencils is _____ : _____ .

3   **a**   Some friends went to the supermarket. Find the total volume of milk and total mass of shopping they bought.

Bought by	Volume of Milk	Mass of Shopping
Mr Lee	4 ℓ	8 kg
Miss Brook	9 ℓ	11 kg
Mrs Smith	13 ℓ	15 kg
Mr Bell	5 ℓ	7 kg
Total		

b   Fill in the spaces below to show the ratios. An example is shown.

i   The ratio of the mass of shopping Mrs Smith bought to the mass of shopping Mr Lee bought is __15 : 8__ .

ii   The ratio of the volume of milk Miss Brook bought to the volume of milk Mr Bell bought is _________ .

iii   The ratio of the mass of shopping Mr Bell bought to the mass of shopping Mr Lee bought is _________ .

iv   The ratio of the total volume of milk bought to the volume of milk Miss Brook bought is _________ .

v   The ratio of the mass of shopping Mr Lee bought to the total mass of shopping bought is _________ .

4 Archie puts some cubes together to form three trains, A, B and C.

a The ratio of the length of A to

the length of C is _____ : _____ .

b The ratio of the length of C to

the length of B is _____ : _____ .

c The ratio of the length of A to
the total length of A, B and C

is _____ : _____ .

5 a The ratio of the length of R to

the length of P is _____ : _____ .

b The ratio of the length of P to

the length of Q is _____ : _____ .

c The ratio of the length of P to the total length of P, Q and R

is _____ : _____ .

6 Draw models to show the ratios.

a 5 : 9

b 12 : 7

7. Grandma Lee gave £15 to Lucy and Charlie. Lucy got £7.

   a   How much money did Charlie get?

   b   Find the ratio of the amount of money Lucy got to the amount of money Charlie got from Grandma Lee.

8. Angus gave bags of fruit to Ben and Kerry in the ratio $8:13$. He gave them the fruit in 2 kg bags. What was the smallest possible mass of fruit Angus gave to both of them?

9. Leanne put 6 counters into a bag. She took out some counters from the bag but not all of them. What is the ratio of the number of counters taken out from the bag to the number of the counters left in the bag? Make a list of all possible ratios using the table below.

Number of Counters Taken Out	Number of Counters Left in the Bag	Ratio
1	5	1:5

Practice 2 — Equivalent ratios

1 Find a common factor, other than 1, of each set of numbers.

   a   4 and 6 __2__

   b   5 and 15 _____

   c   6 and 18 _____

   d   12 and 32 _____

2 Write ratios to compare the two sets of items.

   a

       Group A   Group B

The ratio of the number of CDs in Group A to the number of CDs in Group B is _____ : _____ .

The ratio of the number of CD holders in Group A to the number of CD holders in Group B is _____ : _____ .

_____ : _____ = _____ : _____ in its simplest form.

   b

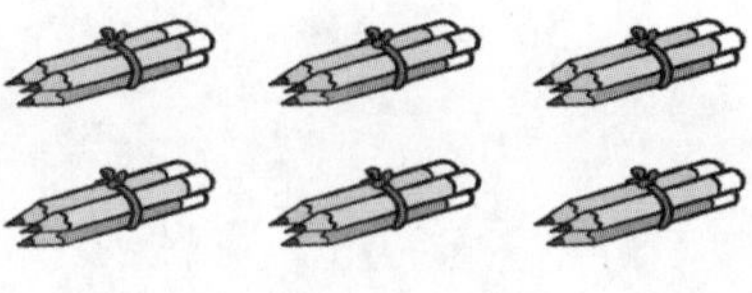
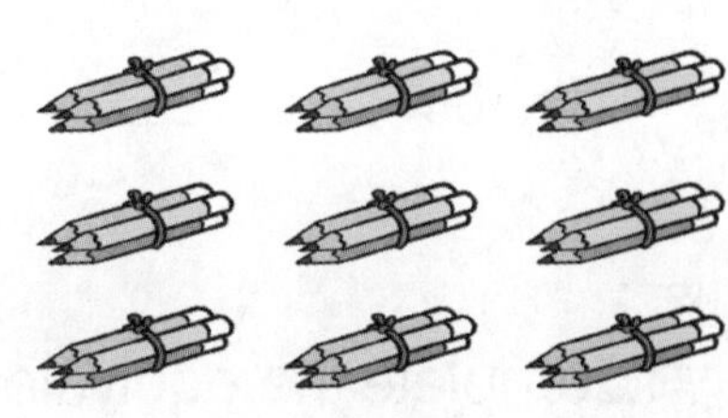

       Group A   Group B

The ratio of the number of pencils in Group A to the number of pencils in Group B is _____ : _____ .

The ratio of the number of bundles in Group A to the number of bundles in Group B is _____ : _____ .

$18 : 27 = 6 : 9 = $ _____ : _____ in its simplest form.

3 For each of the following, find the equivalent ratio.

a 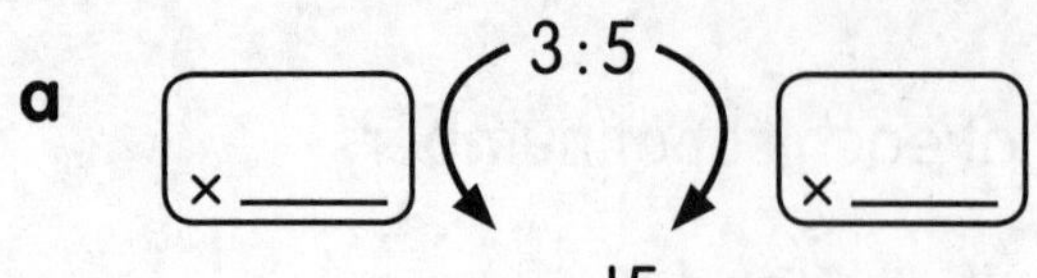

$\boxed{\times \underline{\quad}}$ ⟶ $(3:5)$ ⟶ $\boxed{\times \underline{\quad}}$

$= \underline{\quad} : 15$

b $\boxed{\times \underline{\quad}}$ ⟶ $(7:4)$ ⟶ $\boxed{\times \underline{\quad}}$

$= \underline{\quad} : 16$

c $4:3 = 24:\underline{\quad}$

d $8:3 = 64:\underline{\quad}$

e $4:9 = \underline{\quad}:45$

f $6:7 = 42:\underline{\quad}$

g $5:8 = 45:\underline{\quad}$

h $9:6 = \underline{\quad}:54$

4 Write each ratio in its simplest form.

a $\boxed{\div \underline{\quad}}$ ⟶ $(18:12)$ ⟶ $\boxed{\div \underline{\quad}}$

$= 3:\underline{\quad}$

b $\boxed{\div \underline{\quad}}$ ⟶ $(15:21)$ ⟶ $\boxed{\div \underline{\quad}}$

$= 5:\underline{\quad}$

c $12:30 = \underline{\quad}:5$

d $14:28 = 1:\underline{\quad}$

e $6:16 = \underline{\quad}:\underline{\quad}$

f $15:35 = \underline{\quad}:\underline{\quad}$

g $4:48 = \underline{\quad}:\underline{\quad}$

h $56:21 = \underline{\quad}:\underline{\quad}$

5 Complete the equivalent ratios.

a $5:4 = 25:\underline{\quad}$

b $4:7 = 36:\underline{\quad}$

c $3:8 = \underline{\quad}:104$

d $7:9 = \underline{\quad}:108$

e $48:44 = \underline{\quad}:11$

f $60:45 = \underline{\quad}:9$

g $132:96 = \underline{\quad}:8$

h $72:104 = \underline{\quad}:13$

Practice 3   Word problems (I)

Solve these word problems. Show your workings clearly.

1. Mr Davis bought 24 raisin buns and 18 plain buns for the class party. Find the ratio of the number of raisin buns to the total number of buns Mr Davis bought.

2. There were 44 chicken and fish pies altogether in a freezer. If there were 12 chicken pies, what was the ratio of the number of chicken pies to the number of fish pies in the freezer?

3 There were 12 boys and 18 girls in a class. 3 more boys joined the class and 2 girls left. What is the ratio of the number of boys to the number of girls in the class now?

4 Monica had £42 and Norah had £18 at first. Monica then gave £6 to Norah. Now, what is the ratio of the amount of money Monica has to the amount of money Norah has?

5 In a competition, the ratio of the number of tickets Mrs Elliott collected to the number of tickets Mr King collected was $4:3$. Mr King collected 36 tickets. How many tickets did they collect altogether?

6 The ratio of the number of monster figures Toby had to the number of monster figures Anna had was $7:3$. Anna had 18 monster figures. How many monster figures did they have altogether?

7 In a certain month, the ratio of the volume of water used by Household A to the volume of water used by Household B was 13 : 5. Household A used 455 ℓ of water for that month. Find the total amount of water used by the two households for that month.

8 Some blackcurrant squash and water are mixed in the ratio 4 : 15. The volume of water in the mixture is 1305 ml. What is the total volume of the mixture?

Practice 4 — Comparing three quantities

1 Find a common factor, other than 1, of each set of numbers. An example is shown.

	Set of Numbers	Common Factor
a	2, 6 and 8	2
b	5, 10 and 20	
c	3, 9 and 15	
d	6, 24 and 27	

2 For each of the following, find the equivalent ratio.

a

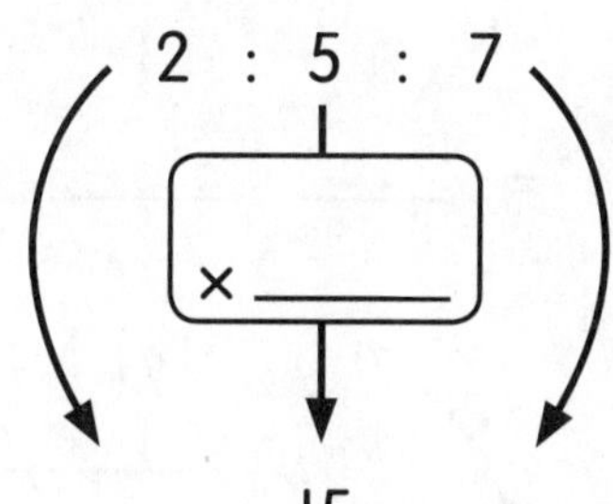

b

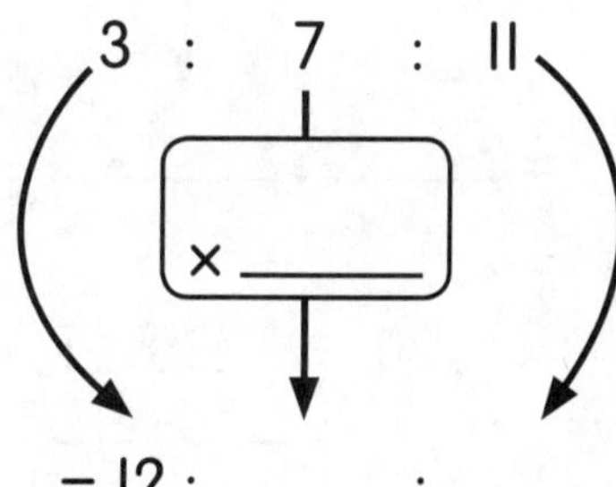

c

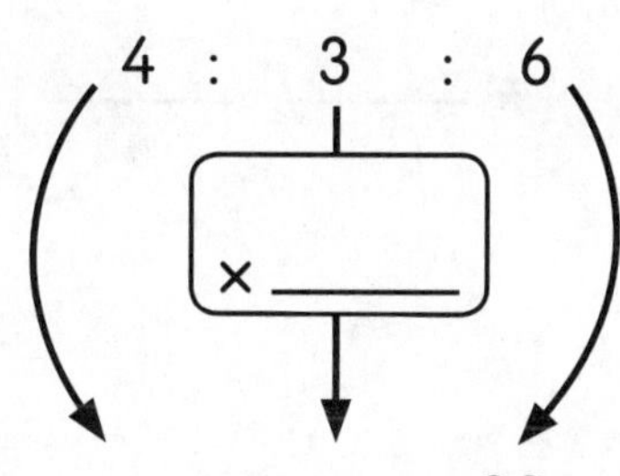

d

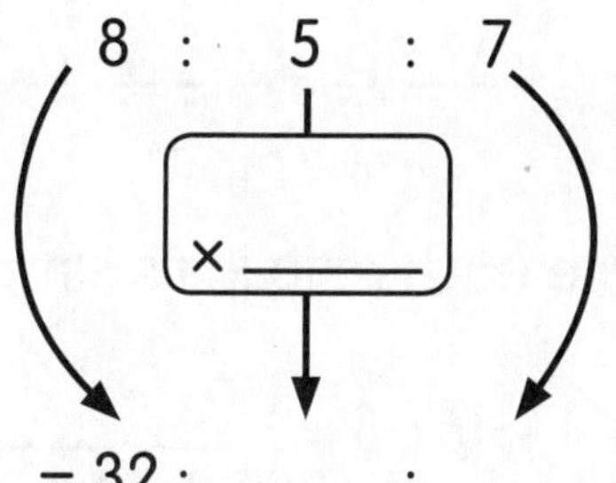

3 Complete each set of equivalent ratios.

   a $1:2:5 = \underline{\quad}:6:\underline{\quad}$

   b $8:7:3 = \underline{\quad}:\underline{\quad}:6$

   c $7:4:3 = 28:\underline{\quad}:\underline{\quad}$

   d $4:5:9 = \underline{\quad}:25:\underline{\quad}$

4 Write each ratio in its simplest form.

a
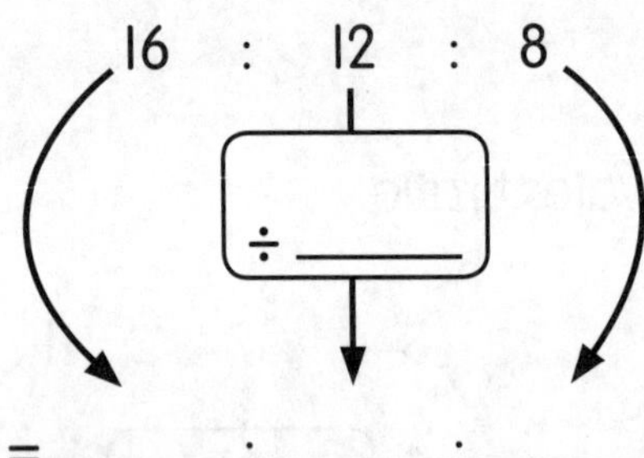
$$16 \quad : \quad 12 \quad : \quad 8$$
$$\div \underline{\quad}$$
$$= \underline{\quad}:\underline{\quad}:\underline{\quad}$$

b
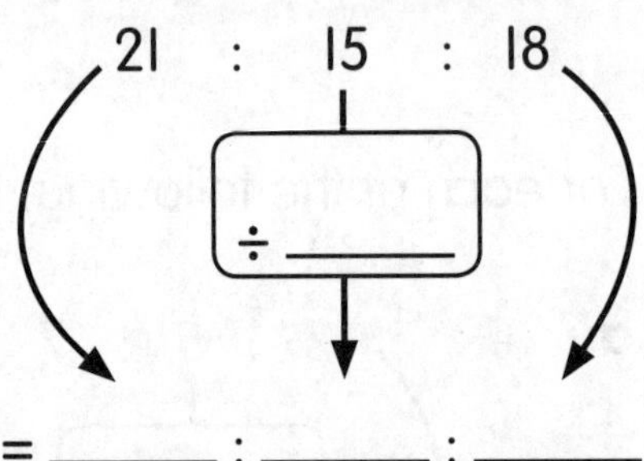
$$21 \quad : \quad 15 \quad : \quad 18$$
$$\div \underline{\quad}$$
$$= \underline{\quad}:\underline{\quad}:\underline{\quad}$$

c
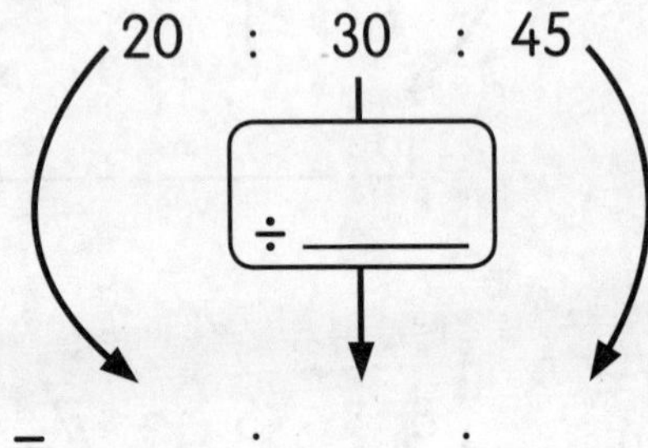
$$20 \quad : \quad 30 \quad : \quad 45$$
$$\div \underline{\quad}$$
$$= \underline{\quad}:\underline{\quad}:\underline{\quad}$$

d
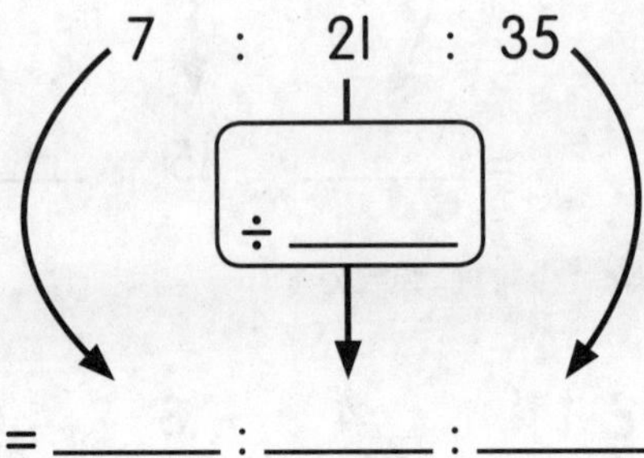
$$7 \quad : \quad 21 \quad : \quad 35$$
$$\div \underline{\quad}$$
$$= \underline{\quad}:\underline{\quad}:\underline{\quad}$$

5 Write each ratio in its simplest form.

   a $4:16:18 = \underline{\quad}:\underline{\quad}:\underline{\quad}$

   b $27:12:21 = \underline{\quad}:\underline{\quad}:\underline{\quad}$

   c $32:8:20 = \underline{\quad}:\underline{\quad}:\underline{\quad}$

   d $63:18:27 = \underline{\quad}:\underline{\quad}:\underline{\quad}$

Practice 5 Word problems (2)

Solve these word problems. Show your workings clearly.

1. Garry bought 4 tubs of raspberries, 10 tubs of strawberries and 8 tubs of blueberries for a class party. Find the ratio of the number of tubs of raspberries to that of strawberries to that of blueberries.

2. Andrew poured 150 ml of water into Container A, 400 ml of water into Container B and 700 ml of water into Container C. Find the ratio of the volume of water in Container A to the volume of water in Container B to the volume of water in Container C.

3 Mrs Thomas gave her 3 friends £900 to share among themselves. Miss Chapman received £200, Mr Hughes received £400 and Mr Bailey received the remaining amount. Find the ratio of the amount Miss Chapman received to the amount Mr Hughes received to the amount Mr Bailey received.

4 Mr Gordon made 750 ml of lemonade. He poured 100 ml of lemonade into Glass A, 400 ml of lemonade into Glass C, and the remaining amount into Glass B. Find the ratio of the amount of lemonade in Glass A to the amount of lemonade in Glass B to the amount of lemonade in Glass C.

5 Ruth cuts a ball of string into three pieces. Their lengths are in the ratio
2:3:5. The longest piece is 35 cm long. How long is the shortest piece?

6 The ages of three brothers, David, Robert and Michael, are in the ratio
1:2:3. David is 7 years old. Find the total age of all three brothers.

7 The masses of three dogs, Boxer, Pepper and Milo are in the ratio $6:4:7$. Milo's mass is 21 kg.

    a   What is Boxer's mass?

    b   What is the total mass of Boxer, Pepper and Milo?

8 Adam, Gemma and Clare collected marbles in the ratio of $10:12:7$. Clare collected 98 marbles. How many marbles did they collect altogether?

9 Amit, Jackie and Tom shared a sum of money in the ratio $13:9:10$.
Amit had £65.

a How much money did Jackie get?

b What was the total sum of money shared among Amit, Jackie and Tom?

10 The ratio of the heights of three buildings, Building A, Building B and Building C is $2:7:15$. The height of Building C is 330 m.

a What is the height of Building A?

b What is the total height of all 3 buildings?

Maths Journal

1 Peter and Miya each drew a model to solve the following word problem.

> A chef bought some meat and potatoes. The ratio of the mass of chicken to the mass of burgers to the mass of potatoes he bought was $3:1:5$. He bought 6 kg of burgers. What was the total mass of meat he bought?

Both their models were incorrect. Explain the mistakes each of them made.

Peter's model

chicken

burgers

6 kg

potatoes

Peter's model is incorrect because

____

____

____

____

Miya's model

chicken

burgers

6 kg

potatoes

Miya's model is incorrect because

____

____

____

____

Draw the correct model. Then solve the problem.

Challenging Practice

1. A small square with an area of 16 cm² is cut off from a bigger square with a side of 6 cm. Find the ratio of the area of the small square to the area of the remaining part of the bigger square.

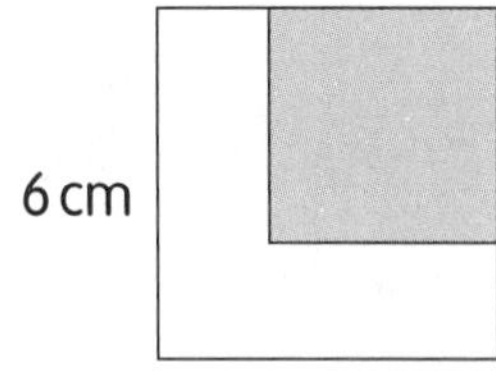

2. The ratio of the perimeters of two squares is 2 : 4. The perimeter of the larger square is 16 cm.

   a   What is the perimeter of the smaller square?
   b   What is the length of one side of the smaller square?

Problem Solving

1. The ratio of the number of plants Mr Hill bought to the number of plants Miss Palmer bought was 2 : 5. Mr Hill bought 16 plants. If each plant cost £17, what was the total cost of the plants Mr Hill and Miss Palmer bought?

2. The ratio of the number of boys to the number of girls at a fair is 5 : 8. There are 60 boys at the fair. If the entrance fee for each child to the fair is £3, find the total cost of the entrance fee for the boys and girls.

Review 3

Date: _______________

1 Look at the triangle below. Name the related height for each given base.

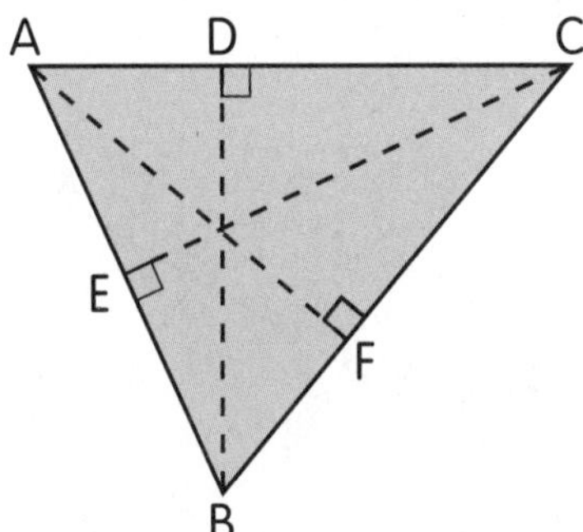

a If the base is AB, the height is _________ .

b If the base is BC, the height is _________ .

c If the base is AC, the height is _________ .

2 Look at the triangle below. Name the related base for each given height.

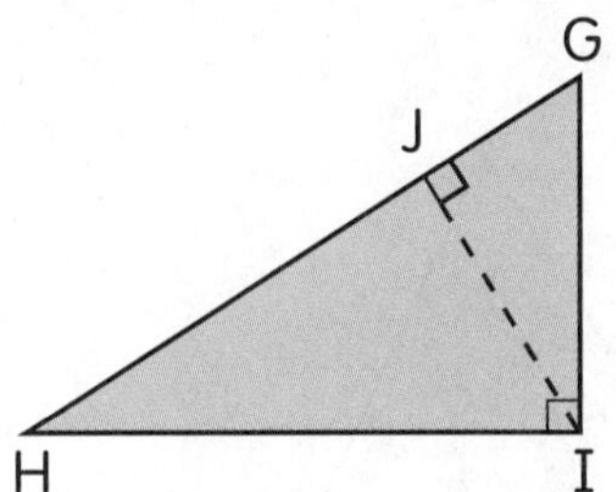

a If the height is IJ, the base is _________ .

b If the height is HI, the base is _________ .

3 In each shaded triangle, a base or a height is given. Name the related height or base.

a

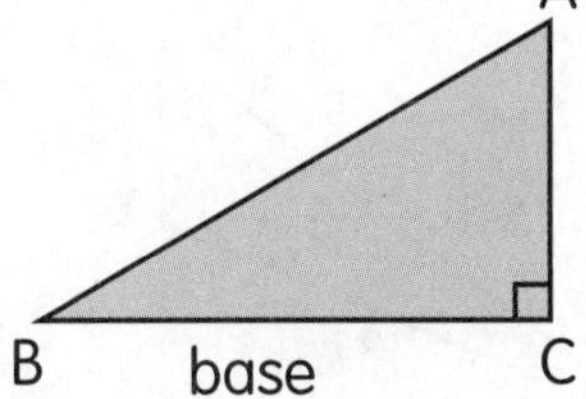

Height: _________

b

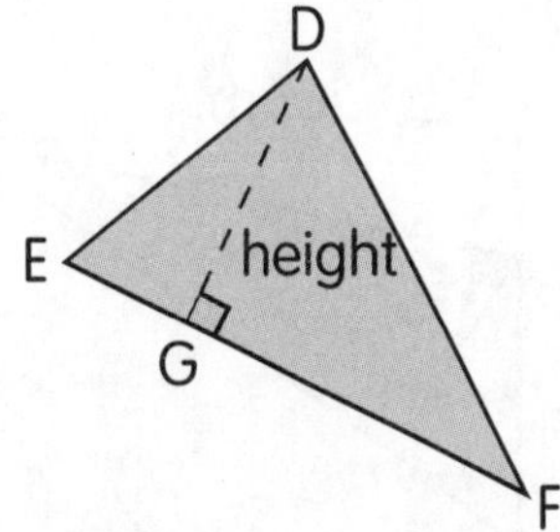

Base: _________

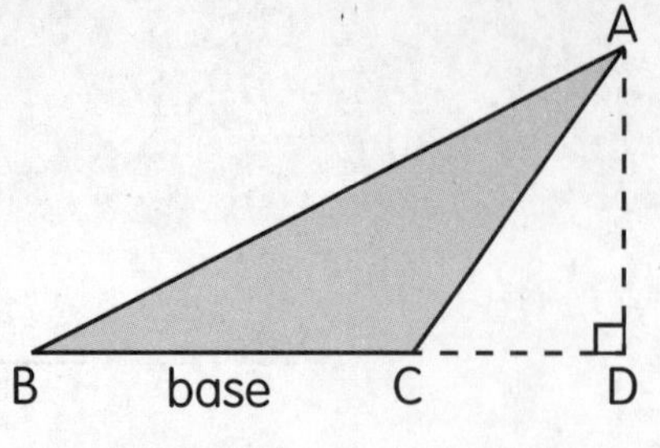

c

Height: __________

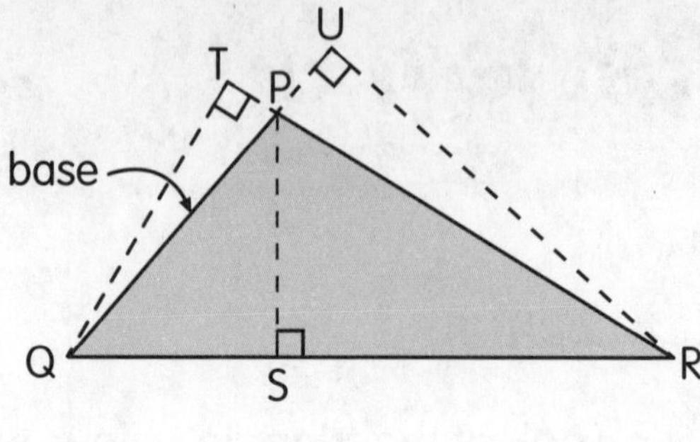

d

Height: __________

4 In the triangle on the right, draw the three heights for the bases XY, YZ and ZX.

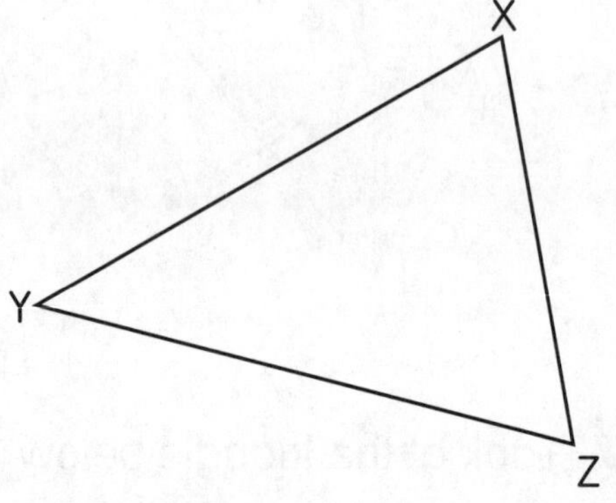

5 Find the area of each shaded triangle.

a

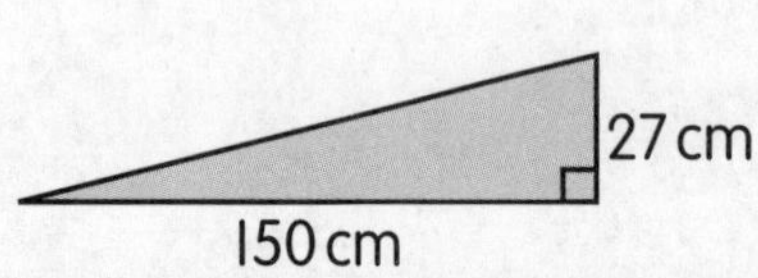

Area = __________________

b

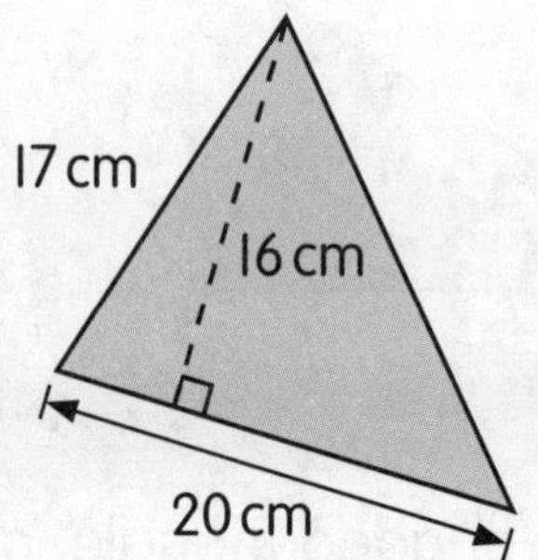

Area = __________________

c

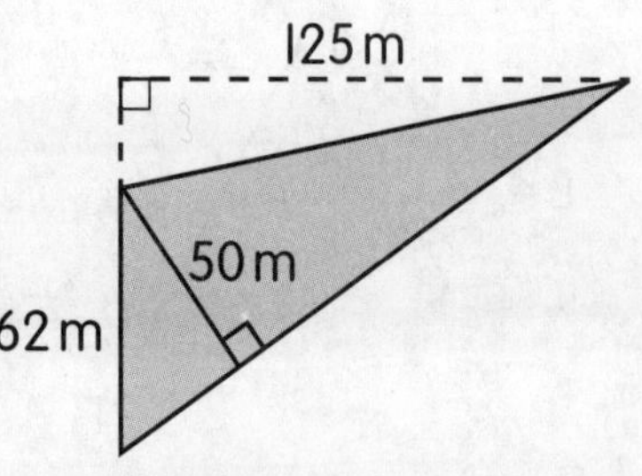

Area = __________________

d

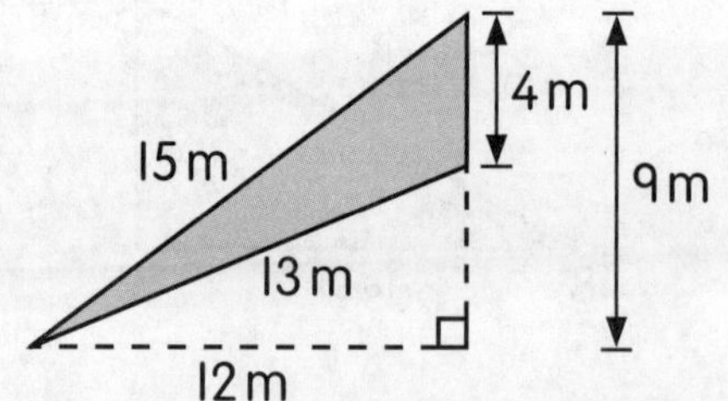

Area = __________________

6 Find the area of each shaded triangle.

a

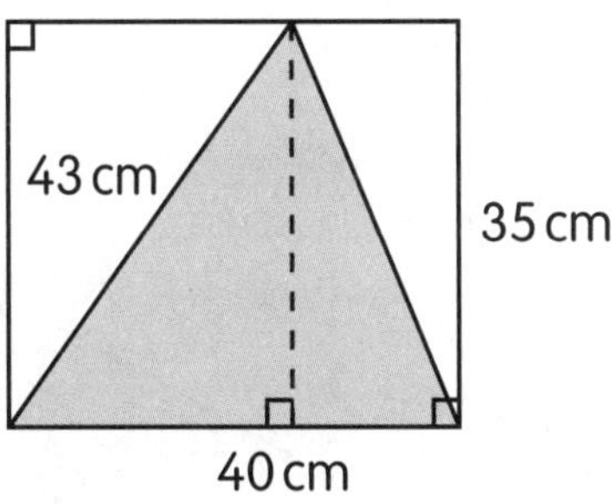

b

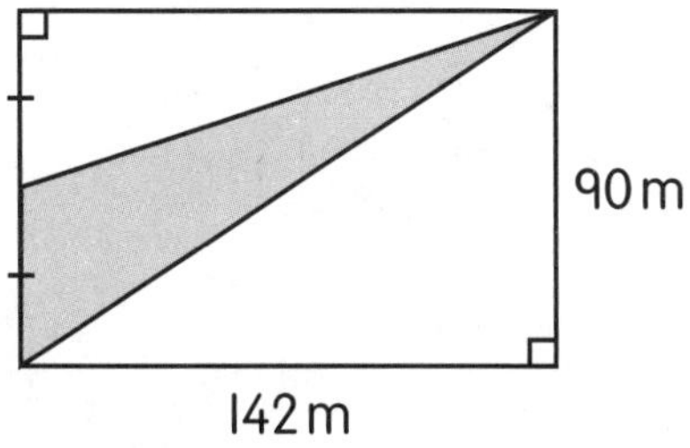

Area = _______________   Area = _______________

7 Find the area of the shaded parts.

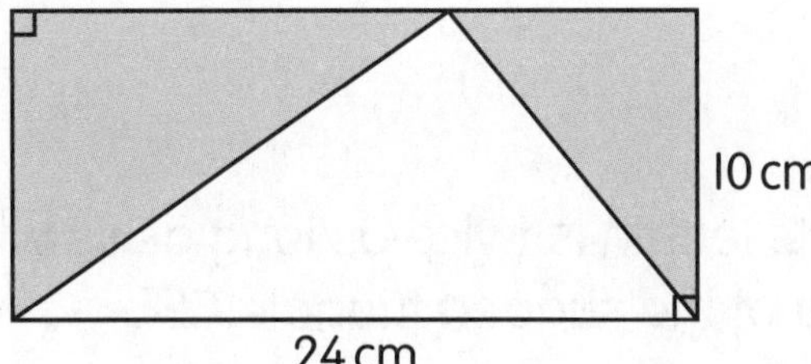

8 PQRS is a rectangle. Find the length of PS.

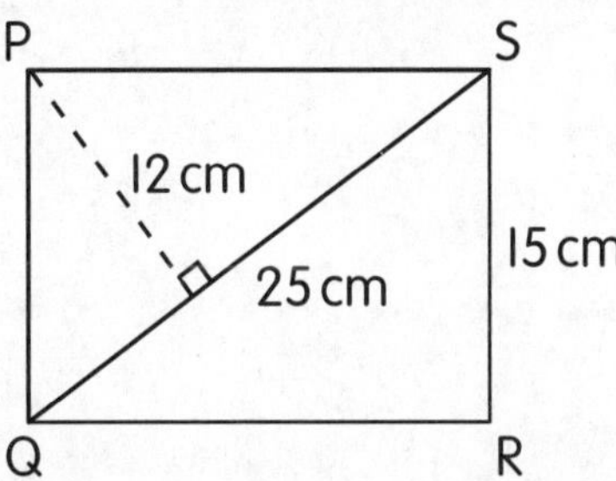

 In the shape, BC = 18 cm and AD = CD. The length of CD is twice the length of BC. Find the area of the shaded triangle ABC.

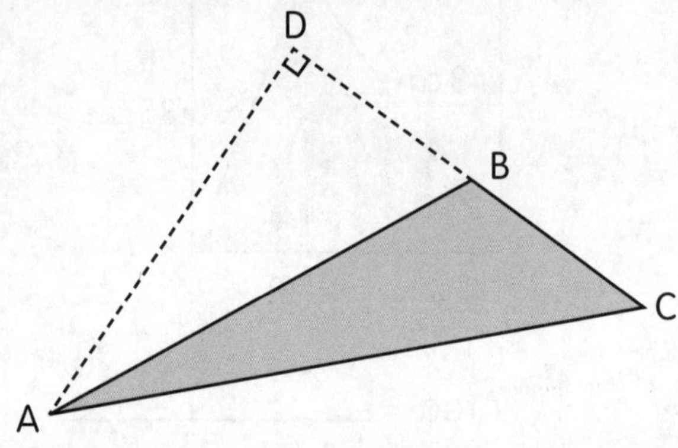

 ABCD is a rectangle of width 12 cm. Its length is twice as long as its width. AE = 12 cm and AF = BF. Find the area of the shaded triangle CEF.

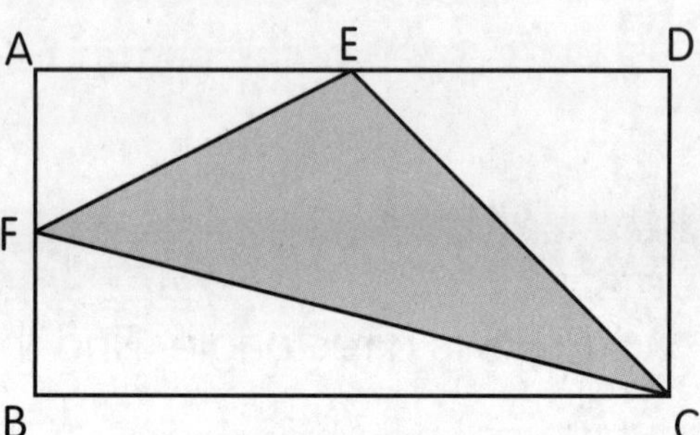

11 Leah used some wire to make a rectangle ABCD as shown below.
The length AD of the rectangle, is twice as long as its width. Find the area
of triangle BEC if she used 108 cm of wire.

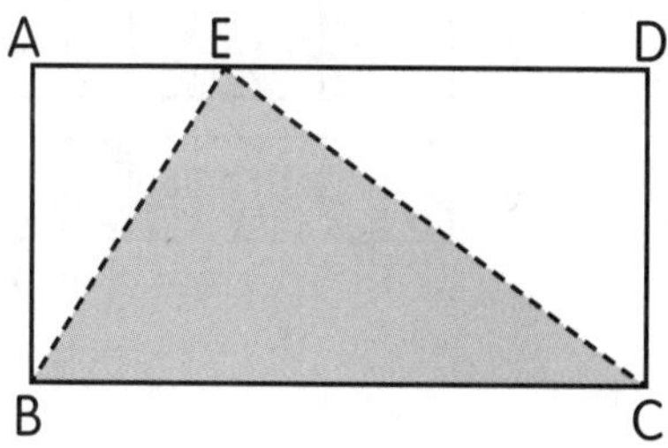

12 Brian drew a rectangle ABCD. He marked points P and Q on the sides AD
and BC and formed two overlapping triangles AQD and BPC as shown.
AP = PD and BQ = QC. He then coloured triangle AQD yellow and triangle
BPC blue. The overlapping region appeared green in colour. What fraction
of the area of the rectangle is the area of the green part?

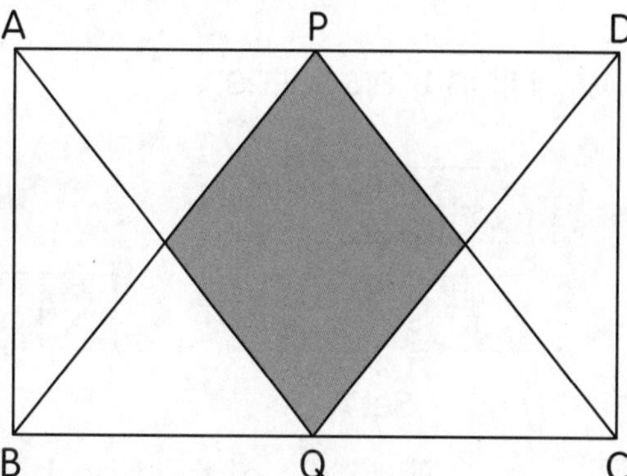

13 Fill in the spaces.

A

B

C

a The ratio of the length of A to the length of B is _____ : _____ .

b The ratio of the length of C to the length of A is _____ : _____ .

c The ratio of the length of B to the total length of A, B and C is _____ : _____ .

14 Christopher had 5 coins in his savings box. He took out a few coins from the savings box but not all of them. What is the ratio of the number of coins taken out to the number of coins left in his savings box? Make a list of all possible ratios using the table below.

Number of Coins Taken Out	Number of Coins Left in Savings Box	Ratio

15 Fill in the spaces.

Set A

Set B

a The ratio of the number of groups in Set A to the number of groups in Set B is _____ : _____ .

b The ratio of the number of squares in Set A to the number of squares in Set B is _____ : _____ .

c Write your answer for **b** in its simplest form. _____ : _____

16 A bakery sells custard tarts in boxes of 6. Ethan buys 7 boxes of custard tarts and Paul buys 9 boxes of custard tarts. Find the ratio of:

a the number of custard tarts Ethan has to the number of custard tarts Paul has.

____

b the number of custard tarts Paul has to the number of custard tarts Ethan has.

____

c the number of custard tarts Ethan has to the total number of custard tarts.

____

17 For each of the following, find the equivalent ratio.

a $7:4 = 21:\underline{\quad}$ **b** $5:9 = \underline{\quad}:63$

c $18:21 = 6:\underline{\quad}$ **d** $24:32 = \underline{\quad}:4$

18 For each of the following, find the equivalent ratio.

a $3:8 = 45:\underline{\quad}$ **b** $7:12 = \underline{\quad}:96$

c $12:15 = 84:\underline{\quad}$ **d** $16:12 = \underline{\quad}:108$

e $99:135 = 11:\underline{\quad}$ **f** $108:72 = \underline{\quad}:6$

19 Write each ratio in its simplest form.

a $8:12:24 = \underline{\quad}:\underline{\quad}:\underline{\quad}$ **b** $21:9:36 = \underline{\quad}:\underline{\quad}:\underline{\quad}$

20 Complete each set of equivalent ratios.

a $4:6:9 = 24:\underline{\quad}:\underline{\quad}$ **b** $48:56:28 = \underline{\quad}:\underline{\quad}:7$

Solve these word problems. Show your workings clearly.

21 There were 45 beads in Container A and 79 beads in Container B at first. Sylvie then took 7 beads out of Container A and put them into Container B.

    a What is the ratio of the number of beads in Container A to that in Container B at first?

    b Find the ratio of the number of beads in Container A to that in Container B in the end. Express your answer in its simplest form.

22 Mrs Moore and Mr Morgan bought a camera each. The total cost of the two cameras was £770. Mrs Moore's camera cost £280. What was the ratio of the cost of Mrs Moore's camera to that of Mr Morgan's camera?

23 A company makes yearly donations to Charities A, B and C in the ratio 3 : 7 : 9. It donates £5096 to Charity B in a year.

    a   How much does it donate to Charity A in a year?

    b   How much does it donate to the three charities altogether in a year?

24 The ratio of the number of boys to the number of girls in a camp is 3 : 7. There are 24 boys in the camp. If the camp fee is £50 per person, find the total amount of fees the girls have to pay.

25 The ratio of the number of UK coins to the number of European coins in Mr Cooper's savings box is $9:5$. He has 640 European coins. If all the UK coins that Mr Cooper has are 50 pence coins, what is the total value of Mr Cooper's UK coins?

26 A small square was cut out from a big square with an area of $576\,cm^2$. The ratio of the area of the big square to the area of the small square is $64:9$. Find the length of one side of the small square that was cut out from the big square.

Revision 1

Section A

Choose the correct answer.
Write its letter in the box.

1 What is 3 450 026 in words?

   a   three million, four hundred and fifty thousand and twenty-six
   b   three million, four hundred thousand and fifty and twenty-six
   c   three million, fifty thousand four hundred and twenty-six
   d   three million, forty-five thousand and twenty-six

2 Which of the following numbers is the greatest?

   a   15 265   **b**   93 216
   c   320 182   **d**   320 128

3 Which of the following numbers when rounded to the nearest thousand is 23 000?

   a   22 097   **b**   22 499
   c   23 400   **d**   23 501

4 What is the value of $20 + 10 \times 19 - 7$?

   a   140   **b**   203
   c   360   **d**   563

5 What is 1000 less than the product of 32 and 79?

   a   111   **b**   1111

   c   1528   **d**   2528

6 What is the difference between the values of the digit 6 in 2 300 628 and in 846 150?

   a   600   **b**   5400

   c   5522   **d**   6000

7 Express $\dfrac{18}{24}$ in its simplest form.

   a $\dfrac{18}{24}$ **b** $\dfrac{3}{4}$

   c $\dfrac{9}{12}$ **d** $\dfrac{1}{2}$

8 Express $\dfrac{8}{11} \div 4$ in its simplest form.

   a $\dfrac{2}{11}$ **b** $\dfrac{8}{44}$

   c $\dfrac{1}{11}$ **d** $\dfrac{4}{11}$

9 What is the value of $\dfrac{3}{4} - \dfrac{3}{8}$?

   a $\dfrac{5}{8}$ **b** $\dfrac{3}{8}$

   c $\dfrac{1}{2}$ **d** $\dfrac{1}{4}$

10 What is the value of $\dfrac{3}{4} \times \dfrac{8}{12}$?

   a $\dfrac{1}{2}$ **b** $\dfrac{2}{3}$

   c $\dfrac{5}{12}$ **d** $\dfrac{11}{16}$

11 Which of the following fractions is **not** in its simplest form?

a $\dfrac{3}{31}$

b $\dfrac{4}{67}$

c $\dfrac{7}{98}$

d $\dfrac{8}{109}$

12 The difference of $\dfrac{1}{2}$ and $\dfrac{3}{11}$ is ______.

a $\dfrac{5}{22}$

b $\dfrac{1}{11}$

c $\dfrac{7}{11}$

d $\dfrac{17}{22}$

13 Find the area of triangle ABC.

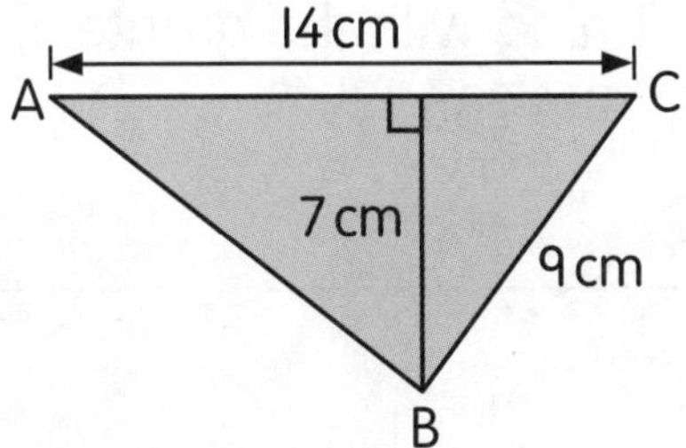

a 126 cm²

b 98 cm²

c 63 cm²

d 49 cm²

14 What is the missing value in the equivalent ratios?

18 : ______ = 3 : 9

a 6

b 24

c 45

d 54

15 Rachel filled a box with 24 oranges and 64 apples. The ratio of the number of apples to the number of oranges in the box is ______.

a 3 : 8

b 3 : 11

c 8 : 3

d 8 : 11

16 Glass A contained 236 ml of milk and Glass B contained 420 ml of milk. Which of the following shows the ratio of the amount of milk in Glass A to that in Glass B?

a 89 : 135

b 119 : 165

c 479 : 660

d 59 : 105

Section B

Read the questions and fill in the answers.

17 $87\,412 = 80\,000 +$ ⬭ $+ 400 + 10 + 2$ _____________

18 Using the digits 3, 9, 2, 6, 5, form the smallest 5-digit even number.

____

19 What number is 32 000 when rounded to the nearest thousand?
Write the smallest possible number.

____

20 Arrange the following numbers in order, beginning with the greatest.

   35 928   164 239   35 982   916 236

____

21 Find the value of $(2 + 4) \times 7 - 6 + 11$.

____

22 There were 215 pupils in a school. The school spent £17 on supplies for each pupil. Find the total amount of money that was spent on supplies for all the pupils.

____

23 Robyn, Sian and Freddie shared a pie in the ratio 1 : 2 : 4. What fraction of the pie did Sian get?

____

24 A piece of string $\frac{9}{10}$ m long is cut into 3 shorter pieces of the same length. What is the length of each short piece?

____

25 On the triangle below, draw the height if the base is AB. Label the height CD.

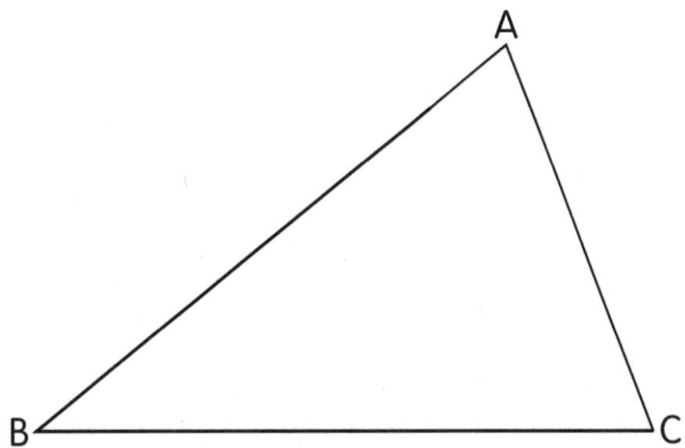

26 Find the area of triangle PQR.

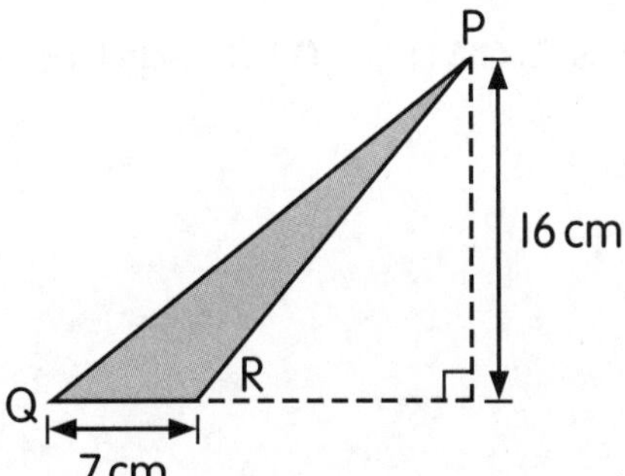

You may use your calculator for Questions **27** to **39**.

27 Express $24\frac{1}{6} - 15\frac{1}{18}$ as a decimal, correct to I decimal place.

28 Find the area of the triangle DEF.

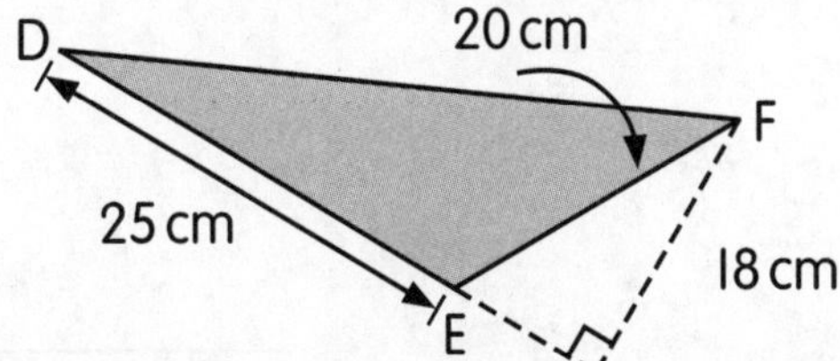

29 Leanne jogged $7\frac{4}{11}$ km on Friday. She jogged $1\frac{3}{8}$ km more on Saturday. How many kilometres did she jog on both days? Give your answer correct to 1 decimal place.

____

30 Find the area of the shaded triangle which is drawn on a cm square grid.

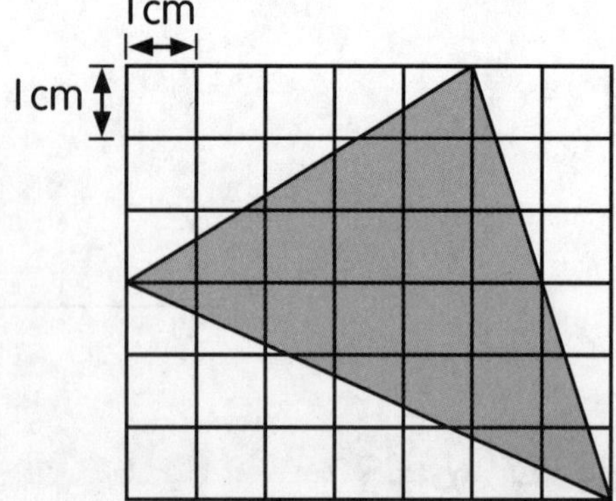

____

31 The ratio of the lengths of three sides of a triangle is $3:4:5$. The shortest side of the triangle is 39 cm. Find the perimeter of the triangle.

____

32 Mr Nelson wants to buy a flat which costs £145 800. He pays £45 000 for the first payment. He pays the rest of the amount in equal instalments for 8 years. Find the amount he has to pay every year.

____

33 The table shows the parking charges at a car park.

7:00 a.m. to 5:00 p.m.	£0·50 per $\frac{1}{2}$ h
5:00 p.m. to 12:00 a.m.	£1·00 per hour
12:00 a.m. to 7:00 a.m.	£2·00 per entry

Mrs Brown parked her car at the car park from 3:00 p.m. to 8:00 p.m. on the same day. How much did she have to pay for parking?

____

34 Box A's mass is $24\frac{1}{2}$ kg. It is $3\frac{3}{8}$ kg lighter than Box B. Find Box B's mass.

____

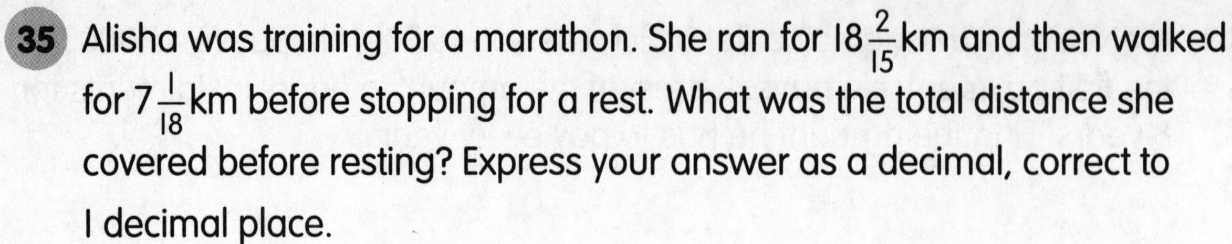

35 Alisha was training for a marathon. She ran for $18\frac{2}{15}$ km and then walked for $7\frac{1}{18}$ km before stopping for a rest. What was the total distance she covered before resting? Express your answer as a decimal, correct to 1 decimal place.

____

36 The ratio of the masses of flour in two bags is $5:7$. The heavier bag contains 1120 g of flour. What is the mass of flour in both bags?

____

37 Rectangle ABCD and triangle XYZ have the same perimeter. Find the area of triangle XYZ.

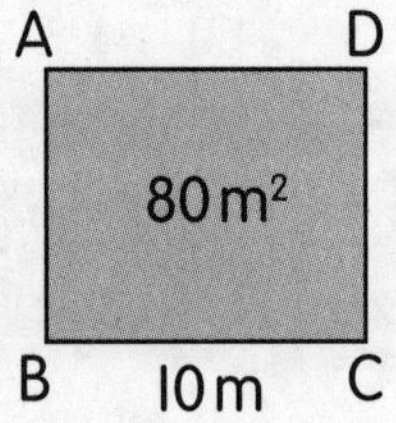

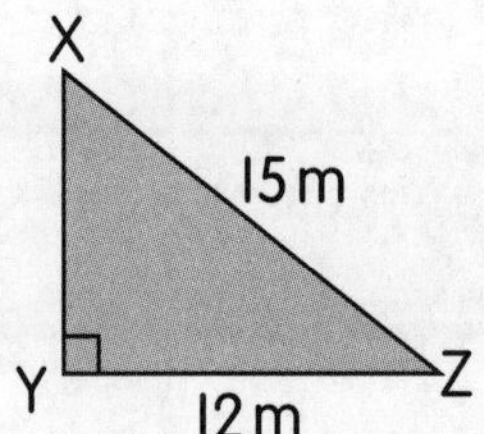

____

38 ABCD and ECFG are rectangles. BC = CF. What is the total area of the shaded parts of the shape?

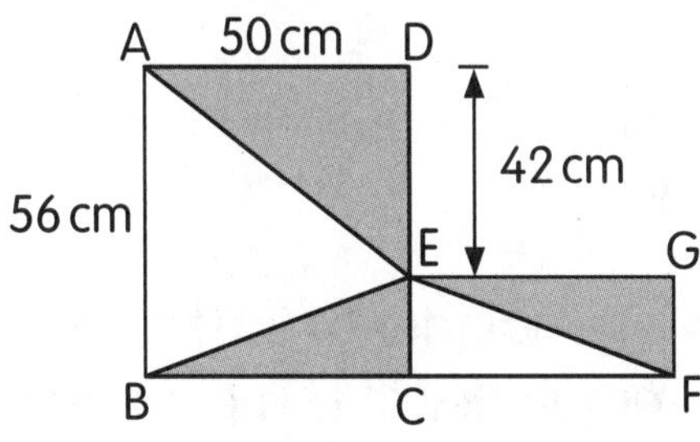

____

39 Look at the pattern of shapes below. Shape 1 is made up of 1 unit square. Complete the table below.

a How many unit squares are there in Shape 4?
b Which shape in this pattern will have 169 small squares?

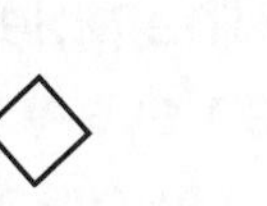  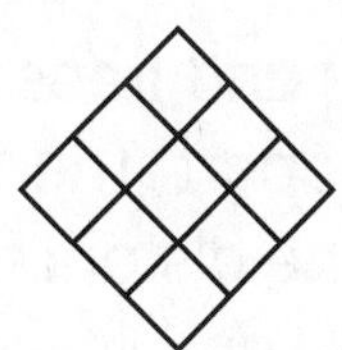 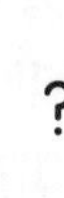

Shape 1   Shape 2   Shape 3   Shape 4

Shape	1	2	3	4		?
Number of Squares						169

a _______________

b _______________

Section C

Read the questions and write your answers in the spaces.
Show your workings clearly.

You may use your calculator in this section.

40 A whole number when divided by 4 gives a remainder of 3. The same whole number when divided by 6 gives a remainder of I. The number is between 70 and 85. What is the number?

41 There are some poles and trees along a 6 km road. The poles are placed at an equal distance apart. There is a tree in between every two poles. The diagram shows the distance between a tree and two poles. Poles are placed at the start and end of the road. How many poles are there?

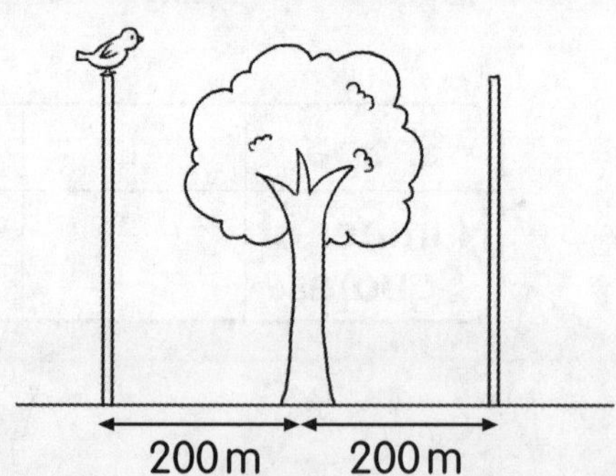

42 Miss Scott earns £525 more than Mr Byrne each month. They each spend £1250 a month and save the rest. Miss Scott does not have any savings at first. After 11 months, she has £8250 in savings. How much does Mr Byrne earn in a year?

43 Mike caught a total of $7\frac{2}{5}$ kg of fish on a particular day. Of the fish caught, $4\frac{5}{8}$ kg were sea bass and the rest were mackerel. He gave away $1\frac{7}{8}$ kg of mackerel. How many kilograms of mackerel did he have left?

44 There were $2\frac{4}{11}\,\ell$ of milk in Container A and some milk in Container B at first. Lisa then poured $1\frac{2}{5}\,\ell$ of milk each into Container A and Container B. In the end, the total volume of milk in the two containers was $10\,\ell$. How many litres of milk were there in Container B at first? Express your answer as a decimal correct to 2 decimal places.

45 Helen had to read a book for her school project. On the first day, she read 72 pages of the book. On the second day, she read $\frac{1}{4}$ of the remaining number of pages. In the end, she still had to read $\frac{1}{2}$ of the total number of pages to complete the book. How many pages were there in the book?

46 Mr Wallace's weekly wage is twice that of Miss Taylor. The ratio of Miss Taylor's weekly wage to that of Mr Franklin is $5:3$. Mr Wallace's weekly wage is £1100. How much is Miss Taylor and Mr Franklin's total weekly wage?

47 The ratio of the volume of water in Container A to the volume of water in Container B to the volume of water in Container C is $2:3:8$. Container B contains 900 ml of water.

   a   What is the volume of water in Container C?

   b   Find the total volume of water in the 3 containers.

48 Look at the shaded part in the square of which each side is 15 cm. P is the mid-point of the square. Find the area of the shaded figure.

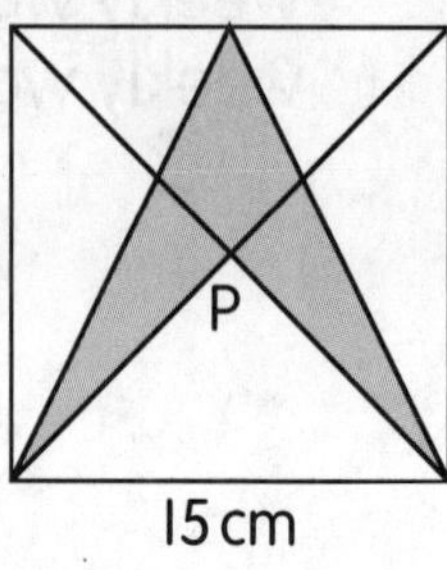

49 In the diagram below, KE = EL, AE = ED and BC is 3 times the length of KB. The area of rectangle ABCD is 90 cm^2 and the area of triangle KGB is 6 cm^2. Find the area of triangle KEL.

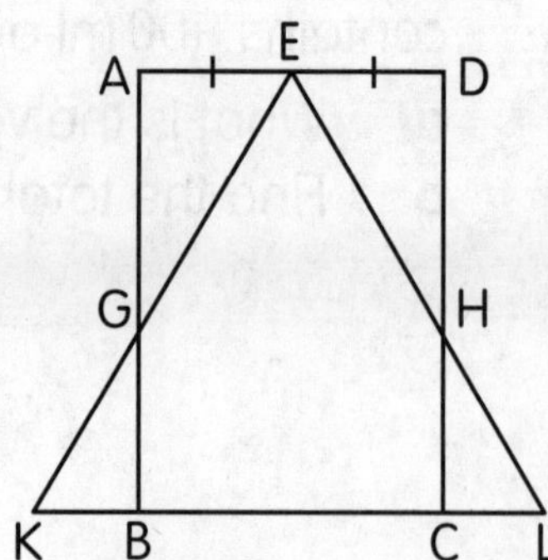